THE
·TRAINS·
WE LOVED

The Bristolian

The year is 1959 and in July Warship diesel-hydraulics will take over from steam power on the Bristolian—but for now steam is king. Bath Road 'Castle' No 5078 Beaufort is ready for a fast run up to Paddington. A west to north train awaits departure in charge of a London Midland 'Patriot' No 45509 The Derbyshire Yeomanry while in the centre road a local Pannier tank idles between duties. The magnificent roof of Bristol Temple Meads still remains and

has in fact been restored in recent years although this particular view has been ruined by the appearance of an ugly Royal Mail bridge at the London end of the platforms. Train-spotters were an ever-present feature at stations large and small and the artist has included two of the breed who are noting down their latest 'cops'. Their inclusion also serves to add scale and a certain majesty to the locomotives and the imposing surroundings. Station pigeons complete the scene.

THE ·TRAINS· WE LOVED

DAVID ST JOHN THOMAS & PATRICK WHITEHOUSE

With 32 paintings
by PHILIP HAWKINS

David & Charles

ACKNOWLEDGEMENTS

Most of the text is by David St John Thomas and much of it based on his personal memories of extensive travel during his early years as a journalist. Patrick Whitehouse had, however, sketched out four chapters (his very last writing) before his sad death in June 1993. Early Memories of Two Lines to New Street and To Beyond Middleton Top are based on favourite reminiscences, while Joint Ventures is the retelling of a vivid tale of years ago. The chapter on Ireland is a compilation of recollections of many happy visits. On one such journey to the Tralee & Dingle Patrick met John Powell, who for the last decade has been an active member of the team supporting the two authors. Alas John also died in 1993, and before preparing his usual contribution to the joint titles. He had however helped in the planning of this book designed to evoke the many and varied aspects of travel at the end of the steam era. One of the most compelling attractions in those days was the Trent Valley. While most young Midland enthusiasts went to Tamworth, Chris Jones shows why other locations also had their devotees. The Millbrook House team who helped see the project through on this occasion were John Edgington, David Johnson and John Smart. They were responsible for the black and white illustrations and their captions.

The colour, however, is uniquely the work of a single artist, the chairman of the Guild of Railway Artists, Philip Hawkins. His knowledge and enthusiasm, as some of the captions make clear, exactly dovetails with that of the authors. This is the first time a collection of his work has appeared in a book, and we hope and expect it will create much interest. For those who might like to secure a larger quality print, nine of the subjects included are the subject of Quicksilver Publishing prints (details from The Sidings, 52 Teignmouth Road, Teignmouth, TQ14 8AS; tel (0626) 773288).

The black and white photographs are gratefully acknowledged as follows:

P.M. Alexander/Millbrook House Collection (17 lower, 18, 20, 23, 26, 33, 39, 41, 52, 56 both, 57, 60, 61, 82, 84, 95 upper, 96, 113 both, 160, 161, 182 both, 184, 185 upper, 186 lower); H. Ballantyne (25, 90, 123, 127); H.C. Casserley (149); K. Cooper (169, 170, 171); T.J. Edgington (83, 101, 132); W.L. Good (45); P.W. Gray (29 lower, 114); G.F. Heiron (8); R.G. Jarvis (177); D.A. Johnson (13, 27, 71, 79, 85, 87, 124, 126, 136, 163, 185 lower, 186 upper); C. Jones Collection (73 upper, 118, 122, 179); J.D. Mills (81); C.F.H. Oldham (17 upper, 30); J. Robertson/Colour Rail (112, 143); W.J. Probert (117, 129, 130); E. Treacy/Millbrook House Collection (12, 19, 21, 22,65, 67, 68, 73 lower, 74, 77, 78, 80, 89, 93, 95 lower, 104, 108, 125, 131 lower, 133, 138, 144, 145, 148, 153, 180, 183); E.R. Wethersett (181); P.B. Whitehouse (28, 29 upper, 44 both, 46, 47, 119, 121, 131 upper, 134, 142, 164, 166, 167, 168, 172, 175 both, 176, 178 both); and Millbrook House Collection (43, 49, 97, 139, 141, 165).

A David & Charles Book

Copyright © David St John Thomas, Millbrook House Limited, Philip Hawkins 1994

First published 1994

David St John Thomas, Patrick Whitehouse and Philip Hawkins have asserted their right as authors of this work in accordance with the Copyright, Designs and Patents Act 1988.

A catalogue record for this book is available from the British Library.

ISBN 0 7153 0292 2

Book designed by Michael Head
Typeset by XL Publishing Services, Nairn
and printed in Great Britain by Butler & Tanner, Frome
for David & Charles
Brunel House Newton Abbot Devon

Page six, top **King on the Cambrian**
Today the bridge over Hatton bank plays host to hoards of camera-toting enthusiasts who flock to watch steam specials, but until the end of steam on BR it was usually deserted. The year is 1960 and No 6015 King Richard III is exerting maximum effort in heaving the down Cambrian coast express up the 1 in 110 Warwickshire gradient. The distinct change in colour of the bricks betrays the fact that, during the fifties, it partially collapsed and was repaired with brand new bricks. The King displays the decorative version of the headboard which Stafford Road and Old Oak Common seemed to prefer at this time. 6015 would be replaced at Wolverhampton or, in later years, Shrewsbury where invariably a Manor would take over for the remainder of the journey to the Cambrian coast.

CONTENTS

1	The Trains We Loved	9
2	On Board	19
3	Western	25
4	Winter	32
5	School Outings	38
6	Early Memories of Two Lines to New Street	42
7	Southern	53
8	Stations	64
9	Village Stop	75
10	London Midland	77
11	Spring	84
12	Joint Ventures	88
13	Central Figure	91
14	Eastern	93
15	Paddington–St Ives	105
16	Summer	115
17	Trent Valley in the Fifties	122
18	North Eastern	129
19	Eventide	135
20	Eating en Route	138
21	Scottish	142
22	Autumn	157
23	To Beyond Middleton Top	164
24	Ireland	168
25	Another Route	179
26	Inverness–Euston	187
	Index	191

Opposite below **On Time**

In sharp contrast to the 'competition' across the city centre, Birmingham Snow Hill was a bright and cheery place and remarkably so when one considers how busy it was. The year is 1947, the last before nationalisation, and a King No 6008 King James II runs into platform 7, well on time, with the midday service to London Paddington. Snow Hill became extremely busy in the early sixties when many London trains were transferred from New Street to ease traffic during the London Midland electrification. It was a bitter blow to many 'brummies' when complete closure came in 1971. A new, albeit smaller and far less grand station, was opened on the site in 1988. The painting was commissioned in 1985 by the Birmingham Post & Mail Ltd to commemorate the 150th anniversary of the Great Western Railway.

Above **Birmingham New Street**

The Midland Railway side of New Street retained its overall roof until the entire complex was rebuilt in 1964. It afforded the receptive onlooker wonderfully evocative light patterns as sunlight forced a way through the smoke, steam and general grime. A Fowler 'Patriot' 4–6–0 No 45506 The Royal Pioneer Corps is standing at platform 7 with a train from its home town of Bristol and will be going onto Sheffield, York or Newcastle. For a few years in the late fifties, and until 1962, Bristol Barrow Road shed had three 'Patriots' on its allocation, Nos 45504/6/19. They were among the artist's favourite locomotives and sadness was inevitable when the last unrebuilt examples were withdrawn from service in 1962.

1
THE TRAINS WE LOVED

MORE people talk fondly about their railway than any other recollections, and more memorabilia from train travel and spotting has been preserved than for any other hobby. This unashamedly nostalgic book celebrates the trains we loved—those of our childhood and those that our parents perhaps told us about in vivid detail. It takes its name from one of the most famous books ever produced for railway enthusiasts, written by Hamilton Ellis at the end of World War II and published in 1947 while Britain's railways were still privately owned. But while Hamilton Ellis looked back to what he considered were the Great Days before the numerous highly-individual railways were grouped into four in 1923, our period of fond memory is that on either side of nationalisation, again within living memory for many—and certainly within the memory of our parents. Our aim as authors is to recapture the readers' yesterdays and unless you smell and hear the trains we describe and illustrate as well as recall their individual character and performance we shall have failed in our task.

We do, however, have some claim to success: well over a quarter of a million copies of the other twelve volumes under our joint authorship have been sold, and indeed much is owed to reader participation in providing material. Sadly, this was to be the last work on which we worked together: Patrick Whitehouse, my partner, died shortly after writing his first contributions to the following pages. Any partnership that lasts for a dozen major titles was clearly solidly based, and his companionship, encouragement and constructive criticism are much missed. The completion of this book, which was conceived appropriately enough on a stroll along the Sea Wall from Teignmouth to near the entrance to Parson's Tunnel, is in large measure a tribute to Patrick who in words and pictures, and in his major contribution to the railway preservation movement, did so much to keep alive the memories of the trains we loved.

Occasionally I have had to ask myself if we were mad in having such affection for them, and also question whether our period straddling but mainly after World War II actually included the Great Days. In presenting the picture as truthfully as possible, it has been necessary to point out short-comings like the lousy station work on my own favourite Western Region. Yet not only were these the trains we had, and which took us on just about every important journey in our life, but many of us feel extremely fortunate to have experienced such a rich rail age.

If there was not quite the variety of pre-Grouping locomotive types and livery, it was nearly a decade after nationalisation before the proportion of the total locomotive stock that was of pre-Grouping origin was reduced to a third. Historic relics abounded, some systems being veritable steam

Brand new BR Britannia class 4-6-2 No 70004 William Shakespeare *stands at Stewarts Lane shed, Battersea suitably adorned for working the Golden Arrow, 11am Victoria to Dover Marine.* William Shakespeare *was on display at the Festival of Britain exhibition on the South Bank (at the end of Hungerford Bridge) in 1951 and is seen here still carrying the special exhibition finish.*

Overleaf **The Midlander**
When the artist was growing up in Birmingham during the fifties, The Midlander became a familiar friend as it passed along the embankment at the back of his home in Winson Green. Stanier Jubilee 4-6-0s were the regular motive power and were allocated to Bushbury shed in Wolverhampton. No 45688 Polyphemus *was one of the regulars and is seen here running into platform 6 at Birmingham New Street at the end of a two hour run from Euston in the mid-fifties. In the background at platform 3, a Fowler 2-6-4 tank is waiting to leave with a local train, perhaps for Lichfield, while a Black 5 has its thirst quenched at platform 1. The Rotunda now dominates the centre background. The distinctive Worcester Street buildings above the signal box disappeared during the rebuilding in 1964. With a generous helping of imagination it is just possible to picture the scene today—if one can ignore the plethora of overhead catenary equipment.*

A King's Cross departure c1954. Gresley class A4 4–6–2 No 60029 Woodcock is in charge of The White Rose, the 9.10am King's Cross to Leeds and Bradford express, as it passes under the North London line and approaches Copenhagen tunnel. Sister locomotive No 60026 Miles Beevor is waiting to come off 'Top Shed' and proceed light to King's Cross for The Norseman, which train ran through to Tyne Commission Quay connecting with the Fred Olsen line ships to Norway.

museums. Numerous pre-1923 carriages also entered BR's ownership. *And we had the enjoyment of the more powerful locomotive classes and more comfortable coaches of the Grouping years and the new BR standard classes.* So while there still remained enormous variety, greater power was available and the best trains generally at least equalled pre-war timings often with heavier loads. Many more people travelled of course, ourselves included; our equivalents might not have been so mobile earlier in history. Summer Saturdays saw pressure as never before on routes to the resorts, and new patterns were established, notably with expresses for business people early morning and late afternoon. If anything proved that the railways now belonged to the people, it was the far greater use made of them, especially for longer journeys including sporting and other excursions. And while the war only provided a respite in the erosion of some of the more profitable types of goods, especially food stuffs and manufactured items, such was the confidence that overall tonnage would increase that a whole new generation of marshalling yards was commissioned.

In many ways we were spoilt for choice. You could catch a through train for Manchester from St Pancras, Euston or Marylebone, the latter's finishing its journey on Britain's first main line overhead electrified section. For Glasgow you could pick King's Cross, St Pancras or Euston. Birmingham New Street and Snow Hill were departure points for quite different kinds of trains to Bristol and beyond. The Cornishman from Snow Hill—it started at Wolverhampton (Low Level) and terminated in Penzance with a Kingswear portion—was one of a number of expresses given names well after nationalisation. Their new glamour seemed to combine modern comfort with celebrating the individuality of the pre-nationalisation railway concerned. It is again told in later pages how nationalisation did not mean instant standardisation and how when the Regions were given more autonomy after a few years, the Western regained chocolate-and-cream for its named trains. A lot more trains were promptly given names, the Cornishman among them. They all carried headboards in a way that pre-war named trains had not.

Which brings me to our artist, Philip Hawkins, whose favourite was always the Cornishman, one painting of which adorns our front cover. Like so many others, Philip was awed by the magnificence and variety the steam railways offered, and has portrayed them in their many moods in a way that will surely bring joy to every reader. He exactly reflects in art what the words attempt to do—and who looking at his pictures would deny that these trains deserved to be loved?

Then there were the dozens of extra features the railways then displayed that we have since lost: the pick-up goods, pinning down of brakes by hand at the top of inclines, simultaneous piloting and banking, water troughs, automatic token exchangers and exchange of mail by the Travelling Post Offices, Passengers' Luggage in Advance (PLA), slip coaches (if only on the Western), and vast signal gantries enlivening the approach to most major stations. While change was in the air in nearly all other ways, the railways were utterly traditional and when speed records were made they were usually by pre-nationalisation locomotives. Pullmans were still important, while at country stations shunting procedures and even the type of locomotive and its load had often scarcely changed in half a century.

The closing of wayside stations and the least-used branch lines began well before the war and restarted in earnest soon after, but the drastic effects of

A typical small town station in what was England's smallest county, Uppingham (ex-LNWR) in Rutland. This May 1958 view finds a mixed train, something of a rarity by then, handled by No 41949 an LMS-built class 3P 4–4–2T of basically London, Tilbury & Southend design. The points and signals were controlled by an LNWR open ground frame on the platform. The station is looking very shabby not having been painted since 1921.

Above New Street 1957
On summer Saturdays in the fifties, huge numbers of day-trippers and holidaymakers invaded stations throughout the country to catch excursion trains to the seaside. Here, at Birmingham New Street, the artist has caught the holiday mood with trains standing at platforms 9 and 10 bound for the West Country. The locomotives are Patriot No 45509 The Derbyshire Yeomanry *and Jubilee No 45682* Trafalgar. *The grand roof was, by this stage, rather dilapidated and if anything looks more imposing than it actually was. The typical British holidaymakers' uniform of coats and macs is noticeable and the 'cheap day' poster is a reminder of pre-decimalisation days.*

Opposite above Rush Hour at Rubery
The motive power on view here is a reminder that the Longbridge to Halesowen line in the West Midlands was a joint Midland and Great Western Railway venture. A Tyseley-based Pannier tank No 7402 is running through Rubery station, watched intently by a member of the local canine population, with a workman's train for the Austin car factory at Longbridge. Waiting in the loop with a freight working is an ex-Midland railway 2F 0–6–0. Because of severe weight restrictions over Dowery Dell viaduct, only locomotives with a light axle loading were allowed.

Previous page, below
Barmouth Junction
This junction, like many, was some distance away from the town of its name: across the river estuary in fact. Here were all of the classic ingredients of the country junction station, substantial buildings, an imposing signal box operating plenty of semaphore signals, token exchange equipment and, on summer Saturdays, a steady stream of trains full of holidaymakers from the Midlands and north-west England. In the fifties, a fascinating selection of engine types were involved including Dukedogs, small Prairies, 14XX tanks, Churchward Moguls, Collett 0–6–0s, and Manors. One of the latter No 7822 Foxcote Manor *takes centre stage. It survived to become one of no less than ten such engines in preservation. The station, sadly, has been reduced to a single platform with a 'bus shelter' as an apology for buildings.*

Reassuringly the brooding presence of Cader Idris continues to dominate the landscape.

Opposite above *A Hereford and Worcester to Paddington express ascends Campden bank on 13 October 1956. The Worcester-based Castle class locomotive No 5037* Monmouth Castle *is immaculately turned out and the coaches look equally smart. Being a Saturday, the leading coach, an LMS corridor second, would no doubt have been attached at Worcester possibly for Motor Show traffic.*

Opposite below *The Southern Railway was able to reinstate Pullman trains soon after World War II and the down* Bournemouth Belle, *12.30pm Waterloo–Bournemouth, is seen near Ashurst in the New Forest on 4 April 1953. The locomotive is unrebuilt Merchant Navy class 4–6–2 No 35010* Blue Star *in BR green livery.*

the Beeching Plan were well in the future. Only the narrow gauge seemed to be in terminal decline. However, to some extent the knowledge that the railways were living on borrowed time—in their method of operation or in some cases their very existence—enhanced our thrill. Most of us were too young to know Col Stephens' eclectic Light and narrow-gauge railway empire and to heed his patriotic demand that we take a journey on a vehicle with metal wheels on metal rails into the deepest countryside where you would never have thought there would be any business; but there was far more to explore than we could ever hope to accomplish. Favourites we always had, and hopefully you will re-experience some of yours in the following pages.

As a boy in the last months before nationalisation I accompanied my father to his publisher, Stanley Unwin of Allen & Unwin, who was preparing Hamilton Ellis's *The Trains We Loved*. We admired his colour plates and, while business was being discussed, I read the proofs, especially the last paragraph which perhaps more than anything else made me enjoy and remember the trains of my generation:

'They were the trains we loved; grand, elegant, and full of grace. We knew them, and they belonged to the days when we first gazed on the magic of cloud shadows sweeping over the Downs, when we first became fully aware of the smell of the Wiltshire village after rain, or when we first saw a Scottish mountain framed in a double rainbow so vivid that no painter dare to try and record it; to the days when, unadvised and at random, we discovered and first read Jeffries' *Bevis*. Those were the days when we first looked with uncomprehending pleasure of early boyhood on a beautiful woman in a flowing Burne-Jonesian dress, when we first heard with awed and incredulous delight the music of Elgar, and they were the days when the steam locomotive, unchallenged, bestrode the world like a friendly giant.'

Though our love of trains began innocently with boyhood purity, it did tend to become more sophisticated, encouraged by magazines, railway clubs and a general awareness of what was happening and why. For example, as soon as we were old enough to read our local or regional newspaper we began to note the reports of those numerous meetings of the Licensing Commissioners which decided whether or not to allow yet another motor coach company to carry people to the resorts. We always enjoyed the railway's defence which included telling little details of the traffic. What locomotive went where, and what challenges were being made; keeping up with all this called for a considerable degree of knowledge. We all thought we knew how best to start an express at a station and watched shocked if the wheels slipped. And how stupid to have stopped dead centre and so to have to waste precious seconds backing a foot or so before going again into forward! After nationalisation we knew what the Transport Users' Consultative Committees stood for and were horrified when the Minister of Transport overturned their recommendations that a branch line not be closed since the loss of trains would cause hardship.

Deep down there was a more serious anxiety—that BR were not doing a particularly good job, indeed sometimes a positively lousy one, in getting to grips with the detail in a rapidly-changing world, and in particular that much freight traffic was lost not because there was anything wrong with railways, just their management. Then of course there were strikes which periodically

A typical Midland Division ordinary passenger train on the Bristol line is hauled by LMS compound No 41180. The train of five coaches, four corridor and one non-corridor, is the 5.15pm Bristol Temple Meads to Birmingham New Street passing Westerleigh in May 1953.

halted the trains we loved as they did most industrial activities. It was obvious that neither the unions nor BR were particularly constructive in the matter of labour relations. But you have to view the railways against the general unhappiness of the age. Their best stood out as a shining star in a generally cloudy sky. Again, to some extent our enthusiasm was based on the fact that things had *not* been modernised earlier.

There was one other aspect, the aesthetic as well as technical appreciation, especially of the countryside. We thought the Midland line to Manchester admirably completed nature's great work at places like Miller's Dale. We did not always have to be right beside a railway, leave alone travelling by it, to enjoy it. How we miss those plumes of steam and smoke expressing the progress of a train through the countryside, often emphasising the sharpness of valley curves not fully realised from the rails themselves! What rural valley's railway did not seem as permanent as the river itself and perfectly in harmony with it, to be appreciated and ever looked at—even though the chances of seeing a train while you were going by road were to say the least scant.

Few of us were wholly one-track minded, but our love for the railway and its trains ran with a deep passion. Sometimes the affliction passed as rapidly as it came (and hopefully this book will enable some to relive memories of that vital phase) while for others...

David St John Thomas

18

2
ON BOARD

MERCIFULLY it is generally the things most enjoyed that are best remembered. So childhood train journeys, and those our fathers and uncles told us about, always seem to have gone smoothly in considerable comfort and nearly always with the sun shining! Not surprisingly, each age has loved the memories of its own trains: of the powerful locomotives of their day knitting the country closer together, new standards of comfort and on-board service, and always the element of exploration. Many journeys were memorable simply because they were novel, perhaps taking us to places (or for reasons) that our parents and grandparents would not have believed possible. The point has often been made that the great expresses of yesteryear displaying their destination boards had as little relevance to the population of the countryside through which they passed as today's hardware orbiting overhead in space. They were just better seen.

Many people thought the Great Days ended with the outbreak of war in 1914. Nothing like pre-war normality had been restored before Grouping in 1923 robbed every large railway (except the Great Western and a few joint

The streamlined high speed era is typified by the LMS Coronation Scot, 1.30pm Euston to Glasgow Central. The train consisted of nine standard LMS mark III coaches which had been refurbished, painted in blue with silver bands and fitted with pressure ventilation. It is hauled by one of the five locomotives built specially for this service and painted in matching colours Nos 6220-4.

The up Red Dragon provides a stirring spectacle as it speeds through Badminton on the South Wales direct line. The date is 6 February 1953 and motive power is supplied by BR class 7 Pacific No 70029 Shooting Star, *which retains the first type of smoke deflectors with handrail. The stock is 100 percent Great Western but is finished in BR crimson-and-cream livery.*

lines) of its independence and character. Those who remembered the rich arrays of trains of the pre-Grouping companies always swore that travel (and particularly visits to stations where routinely half-a-dozen or more different liveries were on display) were never again as interesting.

Helped by more powerful locomotives and more comfortable carriages, however, many new standards were set between the wars, the LNER's Silver Jubilee, Coronation or West Riding Limited and the LMS's Coronation Scot representing the best of that era, with aspects of caring for their passengers that have not returned since. Yet even routine travel on the expresses of the 1930s was truly lovable. Each train was its own individual entity, not part of a regular pattern, and had its staff and passengers to match. Graciousness and spaciousness were what we most remember. They had much to do with over-provision, the generous treatment of such few passengers as there were, few indeed compared with today. Not having a compartment to yourself on many services was a positive hardship; when the author's father arrived at Paddington on a summer Saturday for a train to Minehead, he was as amazed as he was upset that not even window seats were available for himself and his bride. Of course he could have reserved space; there just did not seem any point in doing so. He had been a regular traveller on the former Midland's route out of St Pancras, where feather-light trains of five to seven carriages including a restaurant car still had vacant compartments on almost every run. No wonder the dining car steward almost implored passengers to take a ticket from him after tempting them with the menu and a description of alternative sauces the chef would be delighted to prepare.

After World War II normality was far from being restored when again everything was changed, this time by nationalisation. Not merely was the

20

postwar austerity deeper and longer, but with political change and workers less willing to be subservient to their masters there were real doubts as to whether even thirties' standards would ever be attained again. That substantially they were, and in some cases exceeded, came as a pleasant surprise and is one of the reasons why so many of us think of the golden days of train travel as being as recently as the fifties and early sixties, and on some lines into the seventies. The best on the routes were undoubtedly the trains we loved. We loved them at the time, soaking up every aspect of a highly satisfactory total experience, and we have loved them ever since and been upset by many recent developments.

Just what did the magic consist of? The list of ingredients is surprisingly long.

Accommodation was generous, geared more to peaks than troughs. On most long-distance expresses, including virtually all named ones, it was extremely unusual not to find a comfortable seat except at peak times, such as immediately before or after a major holiday. Mid-week, probably over three-quarters of those travelling by themselves enjoyed a corner seat in a traditional compartment, even in third class. Space per seat was as generous as it has ever been, much of the postwar stock having armrests between the three seats each side. Even in the limited 'open' stock around, windows and seating bays invariably matched. The seats were comfortable, finished in the contemporary moquette. The most common BR design had decorations akin to maps of minor railways, the largest of which from memory had sixteen 'termini'. Natural wood finishes were distinctly un-Victorian yet traditional, and the discreet notice identifying the wood used (there was considerable variety) added to travelling pleasure. The disappearance of the once-standard photographs of places on each railway's system was regretted, only a BR map facing a mirror now being provided.

The Midlander, 5.50pm Euston to Wolverhampton, was one of a number of express trains named in early BR days. It is seen here at the top of Camden bank c1957 with Jubilee 4–6–0 No 45733 Novelty in charge. The combination of the BR maroon stock and early BR symbol on the locomotive's tender helps to date the picture. Rather surprisingly the leading coach is ex-LMS and carries a roof board. The tracks in the right foreground are the up and down empty carriage lines.

Third- (later second- and then standard-) class compartments were so gracious that passengers were constantly checking they had not accidentally trespassed into first class. Those who paid fifty percent more for the ultimate luxury suffered just one drawback: the space between the facing seats was so great that only the tallest people wanting to put their feet up could bridge it. Greatly appreciated by the tall and large, it was said that the huge seats of the first-class compartments had been designed for the typical over-sized BR career chap. Small women sometimes complained they could not sit back in them at all, their backs being poised awkwardly in mid-air if their feet touched the floor.

Traditional Pullmans, including many with third-class accommodation especially on King's Cross services, were still in evidence adding further luxury; this was the age when the Brighton Belle's breakfast kippers were much appreciated. Restaurant cars were a motley bunch but generally most comfortable.

Cleanliness was good, and lavatories were never cleaner, at least on the top expresses where a cleaning woman was employed to walk up and down the train ensuring that all was in order, just one of the touches unique to this period. Another joy for passengers starting from London was that trains were ready for loading well in advance, usually at least fifteen minutes, sometimes thirty.

In these pre-motorway and air-shuttle days, the railway had no competition for speed and the fact that services on many routes were sparse was not much of a deterrent. On the contrary, once you were on board your chosen train you had the joy of much longer non-stop runs than can be found today. Indeed, one of the key ingredients of an enjoyable railway journey was the

A Victoria to Dover Marine boat train (presumably 10.30am—see clock) leaving Victoria just before World War II hauled by Lord Nelson class 4–6–0 No 854 Howard of Effingham *in malachite green livery. The coaches all have roof boards and presumably the train conveyed all three classes of passengers as second class was still in use on the continent, and was not abolished until June 1956.*

comforting assurance that you would not be disturbed by the arrival of other passengers for three or four hours and could sit back and relax to the rhythm, enjoying the moist steam-heat and fresh air through the window. Though speeds were steadily creeping upward, few trains travelled for prolonged periods at more than around 80mph, at which point noise increased dramatically. Remember those top lights above the large picture windows with an arrow indicating the limits beyond which they should not be opened to avoid draught? Yet even now some double glazing was being introduced. Sealed windows and air conditioning were a by-product of faster diesel and electric speed and, though now taken for granted, were never popular in themselves. Even few business travellers of the day saw much point in faster speed, reliability being regarded as the key issue.

Though speed and frequency have both increased beyond recognition on the main trunk routes, there is little doubt that given the choice many would prefer the trains as they remembered them, pointing out that much of the benefit of acceleration has been lost through the insertion of far more station stops. Whereas the best trains from South Wales ran non-stop from Newport to Paddington, for example, most now stop at Bristol Parkway, Swindon and Reading. Mind you, in those days there were few express train options between even large intermediate stops on the same route; those making longer journeys merely noted their privileged treatment. Passengers joining, say, the named trains out of London termini were of course making far longer average journeys than is the case today. Conversely, long-distance expresses generally remained much busier to the end of their journeys, with many passengers getting on and off at stops in the latter half or two-thirds, so that if you had a compartment to yourself for the first 200 or so miles you might then share it with a succession of school children, shoppers or workers, each contingent of which helped give trains their individuality.

Locomotive performance was variable. At its best, such as again from

A cross-country express in a delightful setting on 14 June 1952. The Cardiff–Plymouth service is passing Dundas aqueduct on the Kennet & Avon canal near Limpley Stoke hauled by Castle class 4–6–0 No 5082 Swordfish. Although not a prestige train there would still be plenty of seats on this service, unlike many of today's Sprinter services. Note the old-style ¼ mile post on the right.

South Wales to Paddington, it was reliably stimulating, but it was well into the 1950s before the average standard of maintenance matched that of pre-war days and all too soon after that steam went into terminal decline. Coal became an increasing problem, though on some routes more powerful BR standard locomotives—notably the Britannias on the East Anglian run into Liverpool Street—simultaneously raised speeds and loads. On the Southern, Bulleid's Pacifics vastly improved performance. The A4s did yeoman service out of King's Cross before being replaced by the Deltics on top-notch duties.

Much of course depended on the magic trio: the condition of the machine, its fuel and the crew. Supreme efforts were made to attain the best on the most important business services, especially when it was clear that air and road competition was getting serious and was likely to become cut-throat. These were the days when individual drivers and their regular firemen earned reputations for keen performance, and when inspectors and even the Region's locomotive supremos went out on the road to see for themselves and give encouragement. It was the heyday of *The Railway Magazine's* Locomotive Practice & Performance series, and a train running punctually or early would be noted by huge numbers of onlookers as well as travellers and railwaymen. Even without their tell-tale destination boards, whose demise surely ended the real glamour of trains seen rushing through the countryside, on most routes it was easy enough even for farm workers to tell one train from another and instantly to know how it was doing. The fact that major timetable recasts were rare of course helped.

What would surprise us most if we returned to the days of the trains we loved? Undoubtedly the spaciousness and often emptiness. We would be horrified by the long gaps between trains, especially at important interme-diate stations, and by the fares. Without today's cheapest tickets, the average worker had to be at his job for perhaps three times as many hours as now to afford a typical journey. We would be pleased by the lack of on-board distractions such as the endless to and fro around the buffet car; though we might be upset that the only thing between a fully-fledged meal in the diner and taking our own refreshments was a formal morning coffee sitting in the diner. Mobile telephones and personal stereos lay in the future, but more crying babies travelled than today. And though we might not have agreed that the pursuit of speed justified the sacrifices, we would above all resent the extra hour or more taken by most journeys of over 200 miles compared with today.

Yet that leaves out one major factor: the general ambience. In the fifties you felt more adventurous taking a long journey, and were treated with greater reverence. There was an excitement sometimes laced with appre-hension from the moment you planned your journey until you took the last piece of luggage off. The average amount of luggage was of course greater, backed by many more porters. It was the very act of travelling that was more memorable and which in our own memories or those passed down by the last generation makes it seem that yesteryear's great trains only ran in perfect weather through delightful countryside. If that sounds far fetched, just who in his or her memories has it that the locomotive's steam and smoke spoilt the view?

3
WESTERN

ONE evening in the mid-1950s the old Home Service's nine o'clock news contained an item that stirred the enthusiasm of hundreds of thousands of listeners, 'Boys Of All Ages' to quote the GWR's famous advertisement for its publications. It said that the Regions were to be given more freedom especially in such things as liveries, the Southern being allowed to revert to green while on the Western chocolate-and-cream would be restored for named trains. That night many of us went to bed dreaming up new names. The West Briton for the fast Swansea– Penzance service (like many GWR trains an institution that lasted well beyond nationalisation) was not to be, but neither were we disappointed by Paddington's lack of ingenuity. The Royal Duchy (Paddington–Penzance), Mayflower (Paddington–Plymouth) and Cornishman (Wolverhampton–Penzance) were among those whose names soon appeared in the timetable and sported newly-painted chocolate-and-cream coaches. Locomotives displayed newly-designed headboards.

So it was that at the end of the 1950s and into the 1960s, well over a decade after nationalisation, green

The continuing Great Western tradition of BR's Western Region is exemplified here by BR-built Castle 4–6–0 No 7027 Thornbury Castle, completed in August 1949, climbing Dainton bank on 17 May 1958. The Royal Duchy, 1.30pm Paddington–Penzance, was also a product of the post-nationalisation era introduced in January 1955. The coaches are mostly BR Mk1s in WR chocolate-and-cream while the leading strengthener, a genuine GWR vehicle, is in red-and-cream. The problem of mixed liveries was never resolved.

The original King class 4–6–0 No 6000 King George V *makes light work of the ten coach 4.15pm Paddington to Bristol express near Thingley on the glorious summer evening of 5 July 1952. The Bristol-based King has already been fitted with a larger superheater but is still in early BR standard blue livery. By the end of the summer the more familiar green had been restored, much to the delight of GW enthusiasts. A Centenary stock brake third, still in GWR livery, leads the rake. No 6000 is preserved as part of the national collection.*

Kings and Castles hauled chocolate-and-cream coaches in the time-honoured manner. With Kings still in charge of crack expresses after thirty years, it was not so much that time had stood still (it had to be acknowledged that in other fields of human endeavour things had moved forward!) but that normality and permanence were cherished in a world that generally left much to be desired.

It perhaps shows not just how much interest there was in railways, but that this interest was acknowledged by the authorities in another (earlier) nine o'clock news bulletin which had told us how the nationalised railways would number their locomotives. Those of the GWR were all to be under 10000, and would not merely retain their original numbers but also their cast numberplates. So the green *King George V* (blue livery for BR top-line engines rapidly being discarded) was still No 6000, showing off its bell just as it had well before the war. The continuity was indeed amazing.

And in the same way that it was the Great Western's continuity when it was the only pre-Grouping company to preserve its independence in 1923 that led to an unparalleled level of love and enthusiasm, so now Great Westernism knew no bounds. It was as though Keith Grand, the general manager, had been installed at Paddington jointly by God and Brunel. When Grand was reported delaying the departure of the up Royal Duchy from Exeter St David's so that an extra BR blood-and-custard coach did not spoil the uninterrupted chocolate-and-cream, he was seen as protector indeed of the great tradition.

All this had a rather curious effect. The public well beyond those with a specific interest in railways loved it. Indeed the West Country Writers' Association had passed a resolution at an annual conference stating succinctly: 'Bring back our Great Western Railway', which had everything to do with colour and tradition and nothing to do with politics. It was perhaps inevitable that the railway that had been most profitable and most loved in private ownership should most steadfastly resist standardisation. The *esprit de corps* remained the highest in the Western's mainly well-heeled territory, Paddington being the last London terminus needing to employ coloured porters in the days such discrimination was taken for granted. But the rest of BR thought it ridiculous to a greater or lesser extent. How could people be so in favour of standing still? To which Great Western adherents were wont to reply that it was better than going backward, which was what nearly happened on the signalling front.

As is well known, the Great Western pioneered what was euphemistically called Automatic Train Control or ATC. Ramps placed ahead of distant signals sounded an all-clear bell or an alarm hooter according to the indication of the signal which the driver no longer had to see, and if it were at caution the brake would automatically go on. Since the rest of BR did not have this system, someone in high places suggested scrapping it. Ultimately it was of course replaced by BR's similar and rather more sophisticated system, but it says much for the respect it earned that even during the short transition period when there was no protection drivers were said to be much more tense.

Extraordinary though it now seems, BR continued building Castles for quite a few years. Not every preserved engine with a green taper boiler and a shining copper-capped chimney working on today's GWR steam lines ever saw the GWR itself. The last locomotive of GWR design to be built was 0–6–0 Pannier tank to a new design, none of which were really needed and, being limited to Red routes, could not be used flexibly. All the glory of the pre-war GWR seemed to be embodied in the Region which at first was roughly the same shape. In hindsight it is perhaps difficult to know to what extent Great Western worship would have survived but for this decade or more of 'injury time' after things returned to normal following the war and its austerity aftermath. The Great Western many people cherish in their memories was in truth BR Western Region. The Cornishman on our front cover was never such in company days.

What is undisputed is that the Great Western has been more written about, and more of its artefacts have been collected, than any other business enterprise in man's total history. No commercial organisation under any ownership at any time was more deeply loved.

GWR 4500 2–6–2 tank No 4573 stands at Chipping Norton station with the 4.53pm Chipping Norton to Kingham and Cheltenham (St James) on 7 June 1960. It has probably just run round its train as there are no lamps visible. The line now terminated here having once run through to Kings Sutton (closed 1951). Until the outbreak of war it had been used by the cross-country Ports to Ports Express. Services were withdrawn between Cheltenham and Kingham in October 1962 and Kingham to Chipping Norton the following December.

It was renowned for honouring and exploiting its great traditions, being enterprising and fair, providing the safest transport man has ever enjoyed, making profit till the end, and in our memories it was always utterly predictable. How comforting it was to drive down the Wye Valley and see a Pannier tank do the daily shunt in exactly the same manner at the same time of day in the early sixties as it did in the early thirties. At Torre, when identical crashes happened almost half a century apart, the Prairie tanks shunting the vehicles which were run into by a passenger train delayed peak loads of just the same traffic.

With predictability went common sense. The wonderful thing was that when the Great Western

did eventually change something, everyone assumed it would be for the better. Knowing it would almost certainly be for the worse once the Western lost its greatness was perhaps the hardest part. Soon railwaymen who had previously seen the day on which they had to retire as the worst in their lives now calculate how much longer they had to go. Tens of thousands were of course 'let go' prematurely when the loss of freight traffic resulted in huge deficits, but that was not until well into the 1960s when dieselisation seemed to accompany general malaise and decay—though even in dieselisation Paddington managed to go its independent way with diesel hydraulics rather than diesel electrics. Alas, they were never the Kings of the new power.

From then it went rapidly downhill, loyal Great or just Western men, often of the third generation, seeing their job security jeopardised not only by declining traffic but by the new policy of country-wide promotion, and many from less desirable parts making a concerted effort to move in. Regional boundary changes also blurred the image; the loss of

An evening freight waits for the road south into the valleys at Pontsticill Junction station on 19 August 1950. Two class 5700 0–6–0PTs Nos 5793 and 4635 provide the motive power, the latter is still lettered GWR. The Great Western took control of most of the independent companies in South Wales at Grouping and despite the industrial decline of the inter-war years freight continued to provide the vast majority of the area's revenue.

BR standard class 3 2–6–2T No 82034, allocated to Newton Abbot, leaves Goodrington Sands and climbs the 1 in 71 bank at the start of the single-line section towards Kingswear. It was one of 45 examples designed and built at Swindon between 1952 and 1955. The ordinary passenger train contains through coaches, judging by the roof boards, carrying holidaymakers to the Devon coast resorts.

Soaring above the thickly wooded valleys of eastern Cornwall an unknown Warship class diesel-hydraulic B-B crosses the Largin viaduct as it climbs between Bodmin Road and Doublebois with an up express on 4 September 1965. Introduced by the Western Region as replacements for the familiar GWR steam locomotives, the Warships were themselves soon rendered surplus to requirements following BR's decision to abandon diesel-hydraulic traction. All had been withdrawn by the end of 1972.

Great Western 2800 class 2–8–0 No 3804 emerges from Parsons Tunnel out onto the Sea Wall with a down through freight on 12 September 1955. The locomotive, one of the later 2884 series with side window cab, is based at Newport, Ebbw Junction depot (86A) and will have hauled the train through the Severn Tunnel.

Birmingham and the West Midlands was felt especially severely. You no longer left Paddington for Weymouth, Aberystwyth or anywhere on the once-proud main line through Birmingham Snow Hill to Birkenhead.

Western freights no longer had their distinctive guard's vans in the rear—what a privilege it was to ride in one and alternately sit beside the coal fire on the longitudinal bench or stand on the covered platform surveying the world. They were larger than those of other lines. Steadily all rolling stock became standardised. The last GWR coaches, the Hawksworth stock built between 1944 and 1954, were incidentally the best ever and when placed together in a train formation gave a new distinction to Western trains with their sloping roof ends. But uniformity of coaches was rare on GWR or Western, the profiles of most expresses

being decidedly uneven. The Hawksworth coaches were comfortable (first-class seats perhaps only for the tall and stout) but generally the GWR and Western were mean, insisting on seating four aside when three became common even in third class, especially on the LMS. Track, however, the (Great) Western excelled at. It always used to be said that an LMS coach riding on Western track gave the best journey in the world. The more you knew, the more you appreciated the Western's difference. The twenty-five inches of vacuum for the brakes was, for example, unique to GWR and gave a quicker application, while locomotive headlamp brackets were at 90° to those used on other Regions.

Great Western steam is still big preservation business, while the nameplates of Kings, Castles and others not preserved sell for record sums. Even the painting of a diesel multiple unit chocolate-and-cream for GWR 150 in 1984 seems to have sent blood to the head of some enthusiasts. A lady sleeping car attendant grabbed a passenger alighting in the early morning at Paddington and stopped him till he agreed that it was 'a truly magnificent sight'—

just the kind of thing railwaymen elsewhere in the kingdom mocked as being ridiculous. Yet shortly before that dignitaries of all kinds devoted a day to go to Brunel's office, with its outlook across the transept of the cathedral-like roof, to mark the naming of a diesel *Sir Edward Elgar*. Over the next years the sight of this engine turned out immaculately in traditional GWR Brunswick green brought joy to many travelling around the system. But then the celebrations of GWR 150 in 1985 were on a truly grand scale, nostalgic pleasure only a little scarred by the cancellation of steam into Swindon as staff protested about the decision to close its famous works.

Of course there had to be something beyond showmaship and conservatism to engender such deep emotions. There was. It was orderliness, again the *esprit de corps* which enveloped railwaymen of all ranks into the happy family atmosphere. Yet there was the greatest possible gulf between the few crack expresses on which much of the glamorous reputation was built and the humdrum expresses, not to mention all-stations trains which might take the best part of four hours to cover a hundred miles. Yet it was always unmistakably Great Western, and to many of us magic.

For a start it was always clean, something we may take for granted today but was often the exception elsewhere in steam days. You rejoiced in the predictability of locomotives clearly being direct descendants of nineteenth-century machines though most were more than adequate for their jobs; the predictability of lower quadrant signals, friendly staff, pictures in the carriage to encourage you to increase your knowledge of the GW kingdom. And a kingdom it resembled, with its own telegraphic lingo, coal mining, hotel keeping, farming, housing, social life. Not only was it clean but utterly well kept. Some big stations remained wooden disgraces till well after nationalisation, but none was unkempt. Country stations were often the epitome of romance, and even unstaffed halts (of which the GWR was a pioneer) caught the imagination of photographers. To travel Great Western was usually a delight, the well-dressed staff friendly and often delighted to share their secrets.

This undoubtedly is the Britain we miss. We revelled in the decade or more of real Great Westernism after nationalisation, for enjoyment was ever greater in borrowed time.

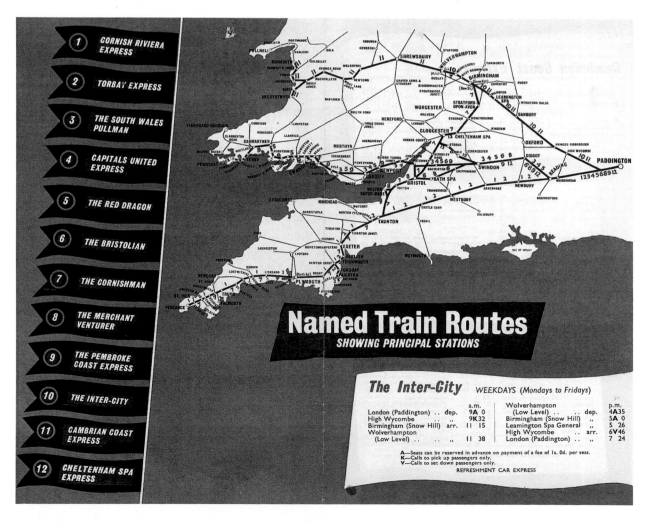

4
WINTER

WINTER of course began as the Christmas traffic was reaching its crescendo and the darkest days were often doing their worst. Most railwaymen took a keen interest in the seasonal traffic, passenger and freight. Nobody's Christmas could happen without their efforts.

Except in years of great fogs, when sometimes trains were so badly delayed that animals had to be slaughtered en route, most livestock had been safely delivered to Smithfield and other markets by 21 December and the only turkeys in transit were those belonging to individual travellers, many to be given as presents, a few to stationmasters and leading porters. Parcels and mail were however still in full flow. These last few days before Christmas were indeed the most difficult of all, mountains of mail delaying the departures of numerous passenger trains while extra parcels and perishables for ever seemed to be on the block.

While many of the famous named trains and also the prime businessmen's trains went their way without Post Office hindrance, delays to those that took all the mail waiting for them were often prodigious. Add bad weather, and cross-country and especially overnight services were sometimes reported so many hundred minutes late that it was hard work to convert it to hours and minutes. Yet it was nearly all good-humoured, with passengers, realising they would be stuck for twenty minutes here and there, raiding refreshment rooms and moving closer to each other to engage in life-revealing conversations. Station inspectors treated onlookers and participants in the loading of mail with equal joviality. In those days there was much more parcel post, and it nearly all went by train. Many specials were run. At Birmingham, for example, the goods shed at Monument Lane was cleared of ordinary traffic and the Post Office took over from 9 or 10 December until Christmas Eve.

Especially before and during World War II, a driver or fireman might descend from his footplate to help stow bags into a leading van. There being much less business (and no 'junk') mail in those days, the Christmas rush was proportionately greater than now. The Travelling Post Offices were of course abandoned, being totally unable to cope and their staff (along with the extra Christmas Post Office staff wearing their own clothes but with an official PO band around the right arm) helped build and demolish heaps of mail bags, often eight or nine feet high on main platforms.

Passenger and goods parcels offices were likewise overwhelmed, every category of their business being busier than usual, but the ultimate pressure was the PLA (Passengers' Luggage in Advance) of children returning from boarding school along with boxes and crates of all shapes and sizes conveying family Christmas presents. Christmas did not start early in those

days; apart from livestock it nearly all happened in the last fortnight. Often parcels offices literally overflowed, a waiting room sometimes being taken over at least for night storage or in country areas crates and boxes being left in the open. An unexpected frost could take its toll, but then slow-moving goods trains offering a much more affordable parcels rate were of course unheated. A visit to one of the large goods stations gave you the very smell of Christmas, and you would see large branches of holly strategically placed for decoration till they were collected and where pieces of mistletoe had been surreptitiously snipped off. Considering the low wages and great visual temptation of just about every seasonal luxury going, from crates of fine port to turkeys and other birds with a label round their neck, the lack of pilferage was a tribute to the railwayman's profession.

The last two working days before Christmas saw the emphasis change to passengers, many of whom were given faster journeys at the last moment than those who thought they would beat the rush but ran into that for mail.

An early member of the GW Hall class 4–6–0 No 4912 Berrington Hall *runs along what looks like newly laid flat-bottom rail track near Dauntsey with the 9.35am Weymouth to Swindon ordinary passenger service on 30 November 1952. The leading vans will probably have been attached at Chippenham carrying traffic from Harris's sausage factory at Calne.*

33

Many expresses were now divided, running in several sections to use railway terminology. Passengers naturally regarded each train as a separate entity, but their crews, signalmen and many others never confused the second or third section of a regular express, with a series of connections to be maintained, and an extra train in the timetable in its own right running just on a few peak days, appearing over Christmas for the first time since the end of the summer season. Each train or even section had its individual ingredients including rolling stock, locomotive, crew, dining car and of course class of passengers. There was, for example, a world of difference between the variety of seasonal atmosphere on board the cross-country service leisurely conveying those visiting distant relatives for the holiday, on trains from the ports with merchant seamen or young matelots intent on instantly celebrating the start of their leave, and on evening expresses from London and other great cities taking exiles back to their families at the end of their last day in the office. Until very recent times, most worked at least until the end of the day before Christmas Eve and indeed a large proportion on Christmas Eve itself.

At the very time that many people used to arrive at their starting station and collect a dinner ticket from the restaurant car steward on the platform outside his car, today things are closing down. Not only did every last evening train run on Christmas Eve, along with numerous extras, but for those not able to leave their jobs until after normal closing time there were the 'get you home' overnight services. Sleepers were fully booked months ahead, many not reaching their destination till well into Christmas Day, when some otherwise closed branch lines ran connecting 'get you home' services.

In England and Wales, Christmas Day services were skeletal, but you could still enjoy the pleasure of a restaurant car meal on most trunk routes, one of the most famous of pre-war railway photographs portraying an LMS chef leaning out of a kitchen car at Euston showing off his Christmas pudding. In Scotland it was of course different, Christmas still being largely ignored and full commuter services running well into the 1950s.

These were the days when main lines never closed, when indeed you woke up on Christmas Day wondering what the separate letter and parcels postmen still had to bring you, and when the collection and delivery of milk and other perishables was never interrupted. That naturally meant that many railwaymen had to work. Staffs were greatly cut, but there was little of the feeling of being hard done by that seems to have grown from the 1960s even though much more was then closed and for longer. Undoubtedly the loneliest were the signalmen in cabins not switched out, administering longer sections with few trains. But then seasonal touches were found in signalboxes as in good depots and restaurant cars. In the days when the same crew always worked the vehicle, and there were no health and safety checks, the more enterprising chief stewards found an investment in paper chains paid handsome dividends in more generous tips.

Christmas did not last 'for ever'. By lunch time on Boxing Day the return rush was gently under way. Some years a full weekday service was run on Boxing Day, but others (especially in the 1940s and 1950s) had an augmented Sunday service with principal branch lines normally closed on

Sundays having a handful of trains, signalmen disappeared from their boxes for the long interludes safe in the knowledge that no inspectors would be on tour. The return rush was less concentrated than the outward one, if only because schools did not restart till the New Year and post and parcels were back to normal quantities. Scotland of course had its equivalent of Christmas at Hogmanay, thousands of exiles boosting takings especially on overnight services from the South. Once again the contrast is notable: when the traffic was again at its busiest, today nothing moves.

And so normality returned, with trains reverting to their shorter winter number of coaches and most passengers being assured of a corner seat if not an entire compartment to themselves. Takings were soon at their seasonal low, milk and other crop yields dropping along with the number of passengers. Yet there were always surprises. For example, the lower the yields, the further milk had to be taken into the big cities, and less went into butter and cheese in distant parts such as the South West. The weather played an enormous part and it is not surprising that railwaymen were among the country's leading amateur meteorologists.

Storms at sea naturally delayed the departure of boat trains from the Channel ports and they halted fish loadings which were the *raison d'être* of some routes, such as the Buchan line from Fraserburgh and Peterhead in north east Scotland. They could also be the railways' ally, for they made life hard if not impossible for the coastal colliers. Storms and freezing weather put more coal, hundreds of thousands of tons more, on to the rails. Despite the huge publicity given to the recent run-down of the coal industry, we forget how recently coal was king, and how regal he was. Each winter enough coal trucks to form a full-length train would be working to supply a larger village; there would scarcely be a single freight yard in Britain without trucks being unloaded. Many will remember the 1947 fuel crisis which hampered postwar recovery and how the BBC Saturday night news reported how many coal trucks had been emptied on that day's special shift so they could return to the collieries for a further load. There was no shortage of coal, just of carrying capacity, with continuing storms halting the coasters while the continuing freeze meant increased demand.

A long freeze upset many patterns. The building trade was slowed down, sometimes brought to a virtual halt, so fewer bricks and other materials were needed. Cement works might close, and quarries (in Cornwall china clay pits) produce only a fraction of normal output. Frosts often happened when Scottish seed potatoes were in transit, many a farmer (usually though not universally fairly) complaining his consignment was useless. The temptation to tap whisky barrels was not always resisted—and if the official allocation of coal for the signal cabin seemed a trifle mean there was always the friendly fireman to ask for a lump or two or even a halted goods train with its inevitable coal wagons to raid.

Our title is of course *The Trains We Loved* and mainly they were the great expresses and country trains of yesteryear, yet it is not surprising that increasing crowds turn up to witness the occasional running of traditional goods trains on the preserved railways. Older readers who travelled in steam days will remember the scene: a handful of passengers waiting for a late train, most of them clustered around the fire in the waiting room, but the more interested pacing the platform listening to the bells in the signal box at its end, or at least emerging into the cold when the signals changed. Surely one of the excitements of travelling by train was that you did not have a visual display of how late your service would be. Expectantly you might hear the approaching steam locomotive, first questioning its slackness but quickly realising that here was another freight whose load would probably be mainly coal going to be burnt in all manner of grates to help keep people warm.

A journey by scantily-patronised express on a crisp, clear day in midwinter was surely travelling at its most luxurious and memorable. Oh, that steam heat! Today we have to pay to enjoy it; once it was free to all who knew how to soak it in. Even when stationary, winter trains were never silent, the hiss of escaping steam that enveloped joining passengers having an almost musical quality. Each compartment had its steam-heating control knob or handle, usually high up on the partition above the seats (or adjacent to the window); sometimes each side had its separate control. The heat released from the broad pipe under the seat was never dry or oppressive. It might send you to sleep as it worked its magic in every pore, but there was no risk of headache or hangover. Steam heat: the very words spell nostalgic magic!

Snow. Falling snow as evil as the thickest fog, prohibiting many shunting movements. Windblown snow getting between the point blades and human beings, with only a brazier to prevent them freezing, doing what point heaters are supposed to do today. Treacherous blizzards closing Highland passes; forcing signalmen to walk instead of cycle between the separate ground frames at the end of the station; occasionally stopping trains in deep drifts, the passengers kept warm by the steam engine until the rescue party broke through. But more often snow the railway's friend, not enough to disrupt it seriously but causing chaos on the roads. Again imagine the scene, this time at a country station.

Normally only five passengers now get the morning service into town and that despite a rapid growth in population. Most of the locals have changed to the bus which starts from the village square, while the incomers drive to their town jobs. Today however thirty to forty pick their way down the footpath across the fields to the station, a few more by the road whose virgin snow has yet to be disturbed by motor wheels. The stationmaster is ready for them. Normally down passengers use the fire in the up waiting room, but this morning the expectant stationmaster has ordered his sole porter (junior at that) to light the fire in the down one, and a nice glow it gives. One and two at a time, the passengers, some of whom have always intended to patronise the train and now feel good about doing so, waddle up to the booking office window and buy their cheap day tickets; they are told 'she' will be about fifteen minutes late.

As the tank engine comes round the curve giving a warning toot the stationmaster leaves the junior in charge of the office to sell tickets to any latecomers and goes over to exercise his skills as social host. If he hopes to secure regular travellers through his efforts, he will be disappointed. Yet in a sense they pay off, for several of the once-in-five-years passengers swear a kind of oath of allegiance to the railway—'absolutely essential for bad weather like this'—and will be supportive in any discussion about its future, in some cases for the next quarter of a century until it is closed.

One of the major purposes of the trains we loved was of course to show us our own country and, since snow made a greater visual impact than any other winter condition, winter journeys were often especially fascinating... by day and by night when there was a full moon and you could expect to see a fox stealthily following the hedge round a field's edge. We were frequently amazed by how much more or less snow had fallen on districts close together, and loved the softening impact of the white blanket on the usually severe industrial landscapes through which trains tended to enter large towns. Often a friend in the countryside but enemy in town, the railway now universally disappeared into the scenery... and at marshalling yards and goods depots you could instantly tell which tracks had been used and which not.

Snow and ice were just two interrupters of the normal winter routine. A particularly exciting one was football specials. Excursion offices and station-masters watched with bated breath to see who would play who and what traffic opportunities that offered. Except where there was heavy commuter traffic (not of course yet described by that name), many stations were used by more special-event than ordinary passengers. In addition to the football there was racing, speedway, boxing, hunting... anything people could be persuaded they needed to go and see personally. The well-to-do still occasionally went by train, the groom riding in the horse box, to distant hunts. Enginemen were asked to keep a sharp look out for hunts in full cry. Special fares were provided for the pantomime until mid-January. Educational specials to places like Windsor and York started up in earnest in the last few weeks of the spring term.

And when passengers came off the last service from the nearest city on a Saturday night, some reeking of fish and chips, and the late-turn porter or signalman went round turning the gas lamps off, there was merriment emphasising that for many social life depended on there being a convenient train. What was next week's film?

But there is one last image of late winter: the evening expresses going to a resort with in almost every compartment a newly-married couple alone. These were the days when the tax system encouraged wedlock before the end of the financial year, and since not every couple could be accommodated on the very last Saturdays the marriage business was on a serious scale even by the beginning of March. In some resorts there were hotels totally devoted to honeymooners before the season proper started, and there we see the Devonian toward the end of its journey from Bradford to Paignton. On other nights there are many empty compartments, but tonight being Saturday the honeymooners are out in force and it is almost as though the number of couples allowed on board has been calculated by the number of compartments. There they are, nestling into each other with what hopes and fears we can only guess, over fifty couples each in seclusion. Who would be a ticket collector on this train?

A typical handbill, measuring 6¼" × 10" produced to advertise forthcoming excursion facilities such as this one to a First Division football match at Roker Park, Sunderland.

5
SCHOOL OUTINGS

TODAY they do it by minibus and have no idea what they miss. The train journeys that used to be standard for school outings are often remembered more than their purpose, which was perhaps taking us to a sporting or cultural event.

They usually required an unholy early start and picked up passengers (it was good to be treated like an adult; they surely do not call you a passenger on the school minibus) at several stations. That involved the first on board not merely bagging the best seats for themselves but protecting others for friends yet to join. Not that sitting arrangements ever seemed permanent, great use being made of the corridor throughout the journeys. Breakfasts usually consisted of sandwiches (of course swapped) washed down by thermos tea on the outward journey. Today's kids would revolt against the weight of luggage that was customary, though things of course go full circle and now back-packing is a fine art. One thing that was never short was space on the racks, above the photographs flanking the mirror one side and map of the system the other.

Wise teachers allowed considerable licence. Even if blocks of seats were reserved, the more adventurous could wander down the train and talk with adults; abductions from trains were unheard of. Or you might get permission to join the mid-morning formal coffee service in the restaurant car, indeed alerting your teacher to its existence though hoping to sit at a quite different table. Two cups of coffee, three biscuits, a shilling: expensive compared to afternoon tea with its sandwiches, bread, jam and cake all for one and sixpence; you had to know that you had to say yes to a refill or you would end up paying the same for just one cup and the biscuits, even though this would still have been thoroughly worth it. You felt on top of the world charging out of your region for maybe only the third or fourth time in your life. A feature of school parties was that almost inevitably some boy or girl was leaving his home county if not home town for the very first time ever.

Windows were for looking out of, and to exercise our independence most of us spent periods in the corridor wondering at the changing landscape and the railway's own organisation. We intended to make the most of the fare bought on our behalf, realising that though we had a real bargain it generally cost more than its *raison d'être* such as a production at Stratford-upon-Avon.

Many school trips involved four or five hundred miles in the day, plus four or five hours at the destination. Adventurous stuff; those making the most of it not necessarily being the cocky ones at school. Train travel surely brought out different aspects of people's characters. Friendships started and ended violently on the way.

The cosiest moment was perhaps when you climbed aboard for the return journey: still hours of movement and independence to go, but the difficult part of being in a strange town seeing something you did not particularly care for now over.

While most school (like Sunday school) outings were by ordinary trains, strengthened when necessary, the excursion departments also put together educational programmes using specials, usually filled by several schools. Not running as part of the timetable and without ordinary passengers, they were never quite as satisfying, though some of their destinations—like Windsor, Cadbury's at Bournville and the 1951 Festival of Britain in London—were genuinely interesting.

The Festival of Britain was especially rewarding. The country was coming out of its postwar misery and excitement was in the air. Walking across the Thames to get to the exhibition gave a special thrill, especially with ceaseless

On 19 May 1950 Castle class 4–6–0 No 4087 Cardigan Castle *tops Whiteball summit with a school excursion. Not only the crew but most of the children also seem to have their eye on the photographer. The coaching stock is in a mixture of liveries including LMS maroon and GWR chocolate-and-cream.*

Southern trains passing within feet. If you got bored with the Festival itself, you could train- and boat-watch from it, steam as well as electric services using Charing Cross whose platforms always seemed occupied. Not that you were likely to get bored at the Festival, for here was a truly magnificent effort to interest everyone.

The railway material itself was enthralling, the large captions indicating we were entering a new era of frequent, comfortable travel for all. Yet back home the Festival made much less impact on family and friends than seems to have been the case back in 1851 when the Great Exhibition had colossal influence. That was the first national event uniting a country thanks to railway travel. Pawnbrokers did grand business advancing the cost of tickets against watches and heirlooms and until our own childhood those who had gone never stopped recounting their experiences. They especially remembered the journey. Not only were they breaking new geographical territory but also experiencing the feelings of independence and exhilaration that only a long railway journey could offer to them, as it did to us.

Why is it that even women who have never been interested in railways still talk romantically about their daily trip to school or the occasional more distant outing? The answer surely lies at least partly in the fact that they were responsible for their own movements, choice of how to spend their time, and enjoyed the respect that any train user experienced. They were greeted by stationmaster, porter, guard as though they were *someone*, and used the station and train facilities provided for all travellers. In realising this, some headmasters and mistresses resisted any attempt to have the pupils forced to sit together in special accommodation. 'If one or two of you insist on being rowdy, you will force me to put you all together and I promise you most of you will lose that precious feeling of independence,' the writer's headmaster said at school assembly more than once.

Boarding school pupils had the different joy of a journey that they would begin or start on their own but of course have other kids on board at the school end. The journey home was always prized, yet even that back to school could be savoured ahead of less happy times. Today's parents who drive half way across Britain to 'save' their children having to endure public transport do not understand what deprivation they are actually inflicting... the same parents who wax lyrical about their own train journeys as though the golden age has ended. And so alas it has in several respects. Fewer places are served by through trains, there is no longer Passengers' Luggage in Advance that enabled everything to be pushed into a generous trunk reliably delivered at school and home three times annually and, whether or not the risks have actually increased, nobody can ignore today's media-hyped reports of molestation and abduction.

However, the purpose of this book is not to pass moral judgement on today, but to celebrate those trains we loved. School trains of all kinds were much loved, are much remembered, and helped make us who we are. Close your eyes and the sun is shining on a neat station as the steam locomotive freewheels in and stops sharply, your desired door of course being exactly in front of where you stand. Always the first impression on getting on the train was its sheer spaciousness. If only school desks were as capacious. Doors closed, you waited for the guard's whistle, the driver's response and the first beat of the locomotive. Homework might still have to be finished, revision always had to be done, yet noting the state of the river or tide or how far the harvesting had gone, or indeed eavesdropping on the conversation of railwaymen, never seemed to be in conflict. While school was inevitably a make-believe world, this was the real one. When you saw neighbours buy tickets to London there was bound to be an appreciative audience if you remembered to tell back home in the evening, and in wartime days of rationing reports of the arrival of, say, sausages at your local station would be instantly acted upon.

School trains were not always punctual. Some provided connections off expresses and might have to wait for their arrival. More exciting were special happenings such as a circus train coming up the incline with engine front and back, the one and only time that was seen. Wonder of wonders, the train was divided in three in front of us: we smelt and heard the animals and joked with their keepers. Each part was trucked into a different siding before our train was allowed into the platform.

During a visit to Swindon Works a party of uniformed schoolgirls is given the latest traction information by the late Burt Stratford, the regular guide around the works. Diesel hydraulic No D604 Cossack, an A1A-A1A built by the North British Locomotive Company works No 25664, was the last of five similar locomotives which were built in 1958 as part of the 1955 modernisation programme. An improved version, the Warship class, was designed at Swindon and a total of 71 examples was built, including 33 by the NBL Co. Two have survived into active preservation.

6
EARLY MEMORIES OF TWO LINES TO NEW STREET

DOWN past Miss Bullows' Riding School you come to Somerset Road. This is Edgbaston, one of Birmingham's leafier suburbs, home to Neville Chamberlain. It is respectable. Go a little further up the hill over Prichatts Road, along past Penrhyn Catholic Preparatory School for Boys and through the avenue of plane trees, peeling bark announcing their presence, and soon you reach the blue brick parapet of an overbridge with a cast-iron notice affixed, a warning by the Midland Railway against excessive loads with the severe penalty of £2 for offenders. On each side of the north parapet are the entrances to Somerset Road station. The western one has the booking office, parcels office, stationmaster's sanctum and porters' room, with an asphalt pathway sloping down to the up platform, serving the line that ultimately reaches Derby. The eastern entrance is via a pair of tall wrought-iron gates leading to a landing berth leading to a flight of wooden steps and a typical Midland lattice-worked wrought iron footbridge, its sides low enough for small boys to peer over comfortably. There is special excitement when standing directly over the tracks with the vibrations, the roar of the train and the smell of coal smoke. This is the summer of 1929 and the station only has another year of life ahead. Edgbaston gentry now have cars; their wives have no wish to walk or wait for trains.

Down the slope with its grassy banks dotted with evergreens, the upper boundary marked with criss-cross wooden fencing in pristine condition, you come to the up platform with its spacious waiting rooms, fires burning brightly from October to May, whether first or third class. Go through the eastern gates and the wooden steps are wide with shallow risers and the down platform is similarly attired though the fence is solid and high. Behind is the towpath of the Worcester Canal where plodding horses pound their slow but steady way towing brightly painted narrow boats neatly lettered 'Fellows Morton and Clayton'. Small boys are not encouraged to listen to the muttered oaths in strong Black Country accents, though nursemaids cock an appreciative ear.

Two miles from Birmingham's vast New Street station, Somerset Road is the second stop out and the first real breathing space for the locomotive crews of the locals. The exit from the great curved train shed is hard, a mile of tunnels up a gradient of 1 in 80, sulphurous and twisting, to Five Ways, the expresses often taking a pilot, usually a 2–4–0 double framer. Sometimes help is given by an 0–6–0 banker, dropping off a quarter of a mile further at Church Road Junction. The goods line from Suffolk Street comes in dropping down from almost parallel tunnels, its busy yard at the far end of the Birmingham West Suburban Railway which originally ran into a terminus at Granville Street before the link to New Street was built. On then past

playing fields to the blue brick canyon of the newly-closed Church Road station, more fields and allotments—very gentrified allotments—and gardens, to Somerset Road where the line describes a concave curve. The station has no crossover or siding and lies roughly mid-way along the 1¾ mile block section between Church Road Junction and Selly Oak. Down stoppers are protected by a somewhat archaic signalling arrangement involving a home signal on a tall post normally held in the off position but put to danger by a porter using a small lever frame on the platform each time a train calls.

Ten trains each way a day call at Somerset Road, the rest snort through on the down line and roll down the up; Kirtley 2–4–0s and 'Hole in the Wall' 0–6–4 tanks from the Redditch branch and Bournville shed work most of the locals, Class 2 and 3 4–4–0s (some oil burners, cylindrical tanks lying in the coal space of their tenders, reminders of the miners' strike) head the fasts though Compounds are now more common. Mr John Selby, the stern stationmaster of earlier times, has gone to his long rest so small boys are tolerated, especially if they have a teenage girl as their companion-cum-nursemaid. The day's highlight is at 4.26pm when a down stopper for Worcester pauses behind Kirtley double framer No 1. But one's mind drifts

Birmingham New Street in 1946 showing the roof over the LNWR side of the station being removed having suffered damage during the war. The platforms had at long last been renumbered, in 1945, in logical sequence and platforms 4 and 5 seen here were both previously platform 2. Number 3 signal box astride the footbridge would be demolished a few weeks later.

43

Five Ways station, the first out of New Street on the Midland line to Bristol, in 1937 with an empty stock train passing hauled by a relatively new class 3P 2–6–2T No 117. A number of these unsuccessful locomotives were allocated to Bournville for Midland Division suburban services, replacing inter-alia Midland class 3P 0–6–4 tanks. The line on the embankment is on the 1876 alignment to Granville Street, original terminus of the Birmingham West Suburban Railway which had been incorporated as a separate company in 1871, and later Central Goods. Five Ways was opened on 1 July 1885 when the MR side of New Street was built and the West Suburban line realigned and connected with New Street through Five Ways and a series of tunnels. Note the Blue Circle cement van based on a GW 'Iron Mink'.

to the sound of an up local sweeping into the station behind what seems to be a huge black engine, almost certainly an 0–6–4 tank, long coaches, likely to be ex-Midland clerestories with red seats, and the deep blue brick walls hemming in the platform.

Journeys from Somerset Road are rare for there is another station almost equidistant at Harborne with more appeal. This is a terminus, it has a turntable and trains linger. There are very many more of them. The walk to Harborne terminus is down York Street, past Bradshaw's stationery and toy shop with its Brittain's farm animals and those glorious Hornby trains in the window and then along Station Road. You are there in about fifteen minutes. Though worked by the LNWR, until 1923 the Harborne line, two miles and thirty-nine chains long, was a private company. Now it is LMS, and the writer's first memory is of being shown the new red coaches.

Harborne is not so posh as Somerset Road, for although the suburb has always been considered 'highly desirable', many of the passengers here come from lower down the social scale. In other words they work for their living, probably from 8.00am to 5.30pm Mondays to Fridays and to 12.30pm on Saturdays. They have no car and even in the early 1930s (the line closed to passengers in November 1934) the weekly season makes the train cheaper than the bus. And as in much of provincial Britain, many season ticket holders return home for lunch if only for twenty minutes. It gives the ticket of just over two shillings real value. There are plenty of trains too, allowing a paternal grandfather to be flexible in arrangements. In the city he posts a card with a penny stamp before noon which will be delivered at 4.00pm announcing his choice of return train.

The terminus lies at the end of a wide sloping drive between rows of better quality terraced houses, privately owned and all likely to have been built

Kings Norton station in the winter of 1934–5 with class 3P 0–6–4T No 2025 on an ordinary passenger train to New Street via Selly Oak. The class was soon to be withdrawn from passenger service following two disastrous derailments at moderate speed. The 3P 0–6–4Ts would have been seen at Somerset Road.

Opposite below A view of the Central Goods branch taken from the footbridge at Five Ways station c1937. Class 1F 0–6–0T No 1700 allocated to Bournville was one of the regular Central shunters. It is not clear from the photograph what is happening but No 1700 may be assisting the freight to Central, although the tail lamp has not been removed from the brake van. The further line is probably on the course of the 1876 Birmingham West Suburban Railway, already part of the Midland by its opening date, and behind the wall is the Worcester & Birmingham Canal. The nearer line was brought into use on 6 December 1891.

along with the railway in the 1870s when Harborne was on the edge of the countryside. Down the road is the fire station, a public works depot for the council and the Chad Valley factory (no planning laws in the twenties and thirties) which has its own siding. This is the magic place where they make soft toys, dolls and above all, for 'Boys Of All Ages', those wonderful wooden GWR jigsaw puzzles. These are cut by young women using mechanical fretsaws, each piece cut by hand. Wages (literally on piece-work) come out at around one pound a week.

Facilities at Harborne station are adequate rather than palatial. The entrance hall has the booking office with its usual barrier opposite the glass-fronted window on the right and a General Waiting Room on the left. Double doors lead from this dingy wooden floored area to the platform which is free to all, and where small boys are accepted if they behave. The great joy of Harborne station is that things *happen*. The goods yard is busy morning and late afternoon with ex-LNWR tanks sorting the coal wagons into the various merchants' pitches and biding their time to move off

Below and opposite *Mitchells & Butlers siding on the Harborne branch, near Rotton Park Road station, which was situated beyond the overbridge, c1947. The Harborne branch trip, target 193 worked by MR class 2F 0–6–0 No 23006, is about to collect the traffic brought up from the Cape Hill brewery by L&Y 0–4–0ST No 11221 which was on loan to M&B.*

between the passenger services. More exciting is the turning of engines and running round the trains. If one is lucky and the engine crews are amenable, it is possible to get a ride. Sometimes the tank engines turn, sometimes they do not. It seems to a small boy to be at the whim of the driver, but it almost certainly depends on the next turn of duty out of New Street. The tender engines, usually LNWR Cauliflower/18in goods 0–6–0s or, in earlier days, Walsall 2–4–0 Jumbos always turn, though these are used only on through trains to Walsall or Lichfield like the 2.59 in the afternoon. The other attraction is the signalman: depending on who is on duty, the single-line staff is either brought down to the loco crew or there is that momentary pause as it is collected passing the foot of the box. The more genial of the two regular men is kindly and explains why the long heavy instrument has Harborne at one end and Rotton Park Road at the other. It is the first inkling of how a single line is worked and sticks in the memory.

As with the ex-Midland side, the departures from the LNWR platforms of New Street are not easy, with the gradient of 1 in 70 starting almost as soon as the trains clear the vast Hill Street bridge. True, the tracks run straight but with a heavy train it can be a struggle. This journey is not over salubrious either but it *is* interesting, for scarcely has one come out of the smoky tunnel when Monument Lane shed appears on the left-hand side. Individual engine numbers are none too visible in the grime, but there is considerable variety here, from Compounds and George V 4–4–0s to tanks from Webb to Whale. Then comes Monument Lane island platform and the carriage sidings

47

before swinging off the Wolverhampton main line with a slowing at
Harborne Junction box to take the staff. Then the regulator opens for the
climb up over the canal, through now closed Icknield Port Road station and
so over 1 in 66 to the summit at Hagley Road. The North Western engine
emits a throaty roar as it tackles the bank, cinders cascading onto the coach
roofs and the grassy cutting sides. One soon learns, painfully, not to put
one's head out of the window. Five and a half minutes from Monument
Lane and nine and a half minutes from New Street comes the one passing
place, Rotton Park Road station, an island platform with the electric train
staff apparatus in the porters' room, levers for points and signals on the platform. Just prior to this is the triangle of tracks for Mitchells & Butlers
brewery, another piece of excitement for the firm has a couple of shunters of
its own including an ancient Aveling & Porter flywheel drive machine named
John Barleycorn. Rotton Park Road serves this main artery at one end and the
busy City Road at the other. It is another good source of passengers as the
buses have not yet taken a hold. To help matters, for a few trains this is the
first stop.

Up once more, still at 1 in 66 to the single platform Hagley Road station
with its small goods yard for coal merchants serving the large houses in the
area. This is *much* posher than Harborne and home to most of the line's first-
class passengers: the station even boasts a ladies' waiting room. Hagley Road
is reached by a tarmac ramp with bushes on either side, the wide carriageway
is lined with trees. In the centre of the road are the 3ft 6in gauge tracks of
Birmingham Corporation Tramways, the railway's enemy. Their replacement by buses in 1930 will spell death to the branch passenger services.

From Hagley Road, it is downhill again at 1 in 66 first through a deep
cutting, then twisting along an embankment once past the bridge under
gentrified Woodbourne Road and looking down on acres of allotments,
more plebeian than those near to Somerset Road station. Over the high
arched bridge at Park Hill Road, a slowing on the curve past the tall home
signal, the dropping of the staff and crawl into Harborne station. All change.
Carriage doors open and are slammed back, tickets collected at the double
doors and the walk home begins.

The child's fare from Harborne to New Street is three ha'pence return,
half the price of the No 4 bus service which is certainly more convenient and
which will, in a short time, conquer. The ideal time to get to the station is
just before 12.30pm as this allows a look at the returning lunch time trains
at 12.38pm, 1.45pm and 2.08pm before a wait for the arrival of the tender
engine turn which forms the 2.59pm out. This arrives at 2.26pm and
Doreen is there to ask if it is possible for her charge to have a ride round. The
enginemen are unable to avoid her charms and it is arranged—the first footplate trip ever. This train is rarely full so it is an empty compartment with
button back seats, a couple of thumps (severely discouraged) producing a
dusty cloud. The train crawls up to Hagley Road, stops, drops down to
Rotton Park, stops again and once more at the disused Icknield Port Road
platform where there is a double arm home and distant signal guarding the
home at the canal curve before Harborne Junction. This stop almost a
normal procedure (as the timetable slot on to the main line is short and their
trains are *never* held) is another nail in the coffin of the branch. Occasionally

the delay is so bad that passengers who have to be back at work jump over the fence and get a tram into town. Eventually the home arm falls and the Cauliflower drops down over the junction to Monument Lane platform, where there is yet another delay while tickets are collected, as New Street is an open station. Off past the shed and down through the tunnel into No 2 platform at New Street where time has been allowed in the working timetable for a prompt departure. The fireman puts the slacker hose into his bucket on the footplate and has a swill down getting ready for the next climb up Gravelly Hill bank and on to Sutton Coldfield, Four Oaks and Lichfield City. It is start stop start stop all day.

Harborne station in LNWR days c1908. A train from New Street is entering hauled by a Webb 2-4-2 tank. The stock is a four-coach 'Inter-District Set' of 50ft cove roof vehicles. The original box, seen here, was replaced soon after the photograph was taken.

Lyme Regis Bound

During BR days, and until 1961, the Lyme Regis branch attracted enthusiasts from far and wide because of its ancient motive power in the shape of three aged Adams radial tanks. They proved to be the only engines which were ideally suited to working this unusually difficult and twisting seven mile route which left the ex-London & South Western main line at Axminster. The painting features one of these old-timers No 30583 wearing BR lined black livery, which suited it well. This particular engine has now been preserved for more than thirty years on the Bluebell Railway.

Halwill Junction

For many years, Dugald Drummond's T9s—known by all and sundry as Greyhounds—were associated with the Southern's North Devon and Cornwall lines. The Withered Arm, as the lines west of Exeter were known, was leisurely to say the least. That most of it survived until the sixties surprised many observers. Halwill Junction would burst into life with simultaneous arrivals and then lapse once again into suspended animation. Time seems to stand still after the arrival of No 30711 with a mixed train for Okehampton in the fifties. The station, actually called 'Halwill for Beaworthy', was some two miles from the village of Halwill, but a new village that grew up around the station was called Halwill Junction—and retains the name long after the last trains called in the 1960s.

51

7
SOUTHERN

THE red carpet has been laid out in a pretty matter-of-fact kind of manner, and indeed it is the third time this week the gang has been responsible for preparing a VIP welcome. Electric trains come and go, some of them (to the expert eye) in fact steam carriages of yesteryear placed on new chassis and provided with electric power: progress with economy. Most are running punctually, but when one arrives six minutes later its driver jumps out and runs the length of its twelve carriages to help catch up time. He is in his front compartment ready for the return, his guard has green flag in hand, eleven hundred people have alighted, a hundred and fifty or so get on, all doors have been closed, and the signal has gone green... all in five minutes. Now that is how a railway should be run.

The passengers (who have been delayed waiting for the late train two platforms away) are perhaps as curious as to what locomotive will bring in the VIP special as to his or her identity. Kings and queens and of course film stars excite interest, but prime ministers of fragments of Empire or mini-Middle East countries attract little attention as virtually nobody has heard of them or recognises them. It is red carpet by protocol, and the officials waiting for today's arrival are obviously second class since nobody recognises them either. Now the special arrives, consisting mainly of Pullman cars. It is in fact double headed, by two venerable 4–4–0 tender locomotives of the T9 class, the lovely 'Greyhounds'.

Still the electrics come and go, disgorging in an orderly manner many of London's best-heeled

workers who cross the gracefully-curved concourse with dignity. But there is plenty of steam, too. Holidaymakers eagerly board a train for the South West; 'Summer Comes Early to the Southern' boasts a poster. And now another arriving train—also mainly Pullmans and obviously from a ship at Southampton—attracts more attention; photographers and onlookers jostle for position as an under-clad yet overdressed American lady, clearly out of the movies, poses as she alights and re-alights, irritating businessmen waiting behind who are no doubt equally rich if less famous. And still the electrics come and go. There is no prize for guessing that the station is Waterloo, jewel among the Southern's London termini, doubling up as international gateway to London and the place where tens of thousands of suburban folk arrive for their day's work... also starting point for West Country and many other holidays. The scene could equally well be in the 1930s or 1950s, and for those of us who enjoyed it after nationalisation—especially after Southern stock regained its green with amazing alacrity—therein lay the magic. Things did not have to be new to be good.

The Southern was, of course, the smallest of the

Overleaf **Evercreech Junction**
This station really came to life on summer Saturdays, as indeed did the Somerset & Dorset in general, particularly during the fifties. Holidays with pay for all came ahead of mass car ownership, but this quickly followed and was the main reason for the line's eventual demise in 1966. Thanks to the marvellous photographs and wonderfully evocative ciné film taken by the late Ivo Peters, the delights of the S&D are widely known and loved. The line's Derby-built 2–8–0s were fascinating engines, quite unlike anything else. The fact that they were regularly employed on passenger duties only added to their appeal. The artist has chosen to feature one of the preserved members of the class: No 53808, which has the assistance of one of the lines 4–4–0s No 40700. Approaching with a train-load of returning holidaymakers is a Southern Region unrebuilt West Country Pacific No 34043 Combe Martin.

An ancient LB&SCR 'Terrier' 0–6–0T leaves the modern concrete of Havant station with the 12.35pm Hayling Island service, comprising a newly repainted LSWR brake composite, on 4 March 1950. It was the light axle loading of the 'Terriers' which allowed them to operate over the wooden Langston viaduct. BR No 32661 had an excellent record of service; built in 1875, it was not withdrawn until 1963, the year the Hayling Island branch was closed.

Philip D. Hawkins

Away from the bustle of the electrified system the Southern could still provide a charm and character redolent of a different age. On the lightly-laid Wenford Bridge line, skirting Bodmin Moor, three Beattie 2–4–0 well tanks Nos 30585-7, dating from 1874, provided the freight service, coupling this with station pilot duties at Wadebridge until their withdrawal in late 1962. No 30587 is now preserved as part of the national collection and No 30585 was also saved.

four Grouping companies. Though there were other bits and pieces, it was mainly made up of three concerns. The London & South Western was the best, and bequeathed the Southern a brand new Waterloo (the best station anywhere in Britain south of the Thames). Many dismissed it as an everyday middle-class affair, without the sparkle of the Great

Rebuilt Brighton class E1/R 0–6–2T pulls away from Watergate Halt on the North Devon & Cornwall Junction Light Railway c1950. The line was constructed as late as 1925 and connected Torrington with Halwill across a remote area of Devon upland, partly replacing a narrow-gauge tramway. Clay and livestock provided the principal traffic with passengers something of a rarity. There were only two passenger trains a day each way along the full 20½ miles of the line. The line formally closed on 1 March 1965.

Western with whom it competed vigorously, though at a disadvantage, in the South West; but it was efficient, ran elegant and comfortable expresses, and made a useful start with the third-rail electrification which the Southern adopted as standard.

The neighbouring London, Brighton & South Coast was so compact that you could traverse the whole system in a day. It spent money cautiously, but had distinctive style, in which Brighton's own traffic played a key role. It had also started on electrification, but of an overhead variety which the Southern discarded.

Then there was the South Eastern & Chatham, not in fact a railway but a management committee running two separate railways which provided the worst services in the land—and gave those visiting Britain via the Kent ports a miserable impression of England. Track, trains, stations, signalling… nothing was up to scratch, but that made the daily achievement of bringing armies of workers into London in the morning and taking them home with reasonable reliability all the more remarkable. There was no money even to think of electrification here.

Somehow the Southern made the best of virtually everything. It has indeed often been described as the most sensible transport system ever run. It was utterly pragmatic. Electrification meant just that; adding an electric rail and electric power, often to existing rolling stock… not the excuse totally to resignal and rebuild that has become standard in more recent times. Old semaphore signals controlled the first generation of electrics, and when the time came to build new boxes with colour-light signalling, the new equipment sometimes went into the old buildings. Where bits of old equipment were still doing a good job, they were retained.

Nothing was thrown away. Steam engines made redundant by the steady electrification programme were deployed elsewhere, making it possible simultaneously to get rid of the really ancient machines (though many Victorian ones survived into BR days) and avoid new building.

The railway was run much along the lines of a family business, the man acting as owner being Sir Herbert Walker, one of the greatest of all railwaymen. General manager of the London & South Western, he had been offered the plum job on the much larger London, Midland & Scottish, but realised the Southern offered great potential.

Walker had no counterpart elsewhere in the railway world. He respected his board but prevented its interference in his domain: the daily running of the railway. His authority was total, his aim crystal clear: electrification. The end product was train miles. The greater number of them, the more services that switched to regular-interval patterns with trains so frequent that passengers need not consult a timetable, the more profit would be earned to afford more electrification... and so more train miles.

In 1923 the Southern ran a weekday average of 130,000 train miles. By 1938 it was up to 170,000, achieved with a reduction in rolling stock and staff. Success lay in smooth routine, avoiding the exceptional. The Southern worked with a rhythm the other railways never achieved. Sections of trains were joined or divided in a quarter of the time the GWR often took, while routinely electrics were allowed fifteen seconds per station, thirty at important junctions.

An up Continental express leaves the 2141 yard Penge Tunnel and runs through Sydenham Hill station en route to Victoria. The boat train, complete with luggage vans, is hauled by Battle of Britain class Pacific No 34074 46 Squadron on Saturday 19 August 1950. The 110 Bulleid light Pacifics built between 1945 and 1951 found work all over the Southern system, from north Devon and Cornwall to eastern Kent. Sixty members of the class were later rebuilt with conventional valve gear and the air-smoothed casing removed.

Overleaf above **Slumbering Giant**

Bullied's Pacifics were distinctive locomotives by any standards, particularly in their original air-smoothed condition. His Merchant Navys underwent many detail changes before being rebuilt into more conventional machines from 1956. One of these engines in final condition is No 35004 Cunard White Star captured lurking in the smoky depths of Nine Elms shed. It is ready for duty at the head of the Atlantic Coast Express, known to railwaymen and enthusiasts alike as the ACE. It will shortly reverse up to Waterloo to join its famous train. Keeping company are two unrebuilt Light Pacifics, West Country No 34092 City of Wells and Battle of Britain No 34086 219 Squadron.

Above **Iron Duke and the Shed Cat**
The world-famous Golden Arrow was the Southern's flagship train with Stewarts Lane shed providing the motive power. The immediate environment of this depot, in Battersea, south London, meant that the cleaning staff had to work miracles day after day to achieve the standard of turnout seen here. British Railways Britannia Pacific No 70014 Iron Duke was one of two of its class to be allocated here from 1951 until 1958 and regularly hauled the Golden Arrow Pullman car train between Victoria and Dover. The fine-looking engine is seen here being prepared prior to backing down the terminus to take out its train.

Opposite below **Southern Freeze**
The winter of 1963 was particularly harsh and affected every corner of the country. Most areas of British Railways managed to keep traffic moving and proved, not for the first time, the advantage of rail over road transport in such weather conditions. How many towns and villages would welcome the return of lines closed during the Beeching years when the winter weather closes in? Devon did not escape the snow, and staff at Exmouth Junction shed did their bit to keep services moving. Battle of Britain No 34072 257 Squadron, in original condition faces a classmate. The duties of these engines based at 72A varied between one and two coach trains along the routes of the Withered Arm in North Devon and Cornwall and hauling fast, full-length trains up to Waterloo.

A Schools class 4–4–0 No 30927 Clifton *heads a Charing Cross–Hastings express out of Mountfield tunnel on 16 September 1952. Both the locomotive and carriages were designed to operate over the restricted loading gauge of the Hastings line. No 30927 carries BR lined black livery.*

Public relations were transformed by the appointment of a rising journalist, John Elliot (who eventually played a key role in general management). Britain's first 'public relations' man, Elliot's remit was total: advertising, the evolution of a Southern 'style', details of uniform, slogans that became household words and posters that everyone loved... the Southern came to life with a sharp personality and became liked by its ever-increasing number of passengers. As train miles went up, concerted efforts were made to persuade people to relocate into Southern suburban land.

In short, the Southern became the world's largest and best-run train set, blessed with considerable continuity and stability despite economic constraint. It was all practice and little theory. What could be sub-contracted profitably, was. Catering and road cartage in most rural areas were sub-contracted, while the railway ran its own quarry, concrete works and much more... along with a substantial cross-Channel fleet whose productivity was steadily raised.

Then there simply was not the money that became available for the grandiose schemes (and mistakes) of later years. Down in the West Country, the workers at Meldon Quarry on Dartmoor might have earned good wages as ballast was needed for more electrification south of the Thames, but the trains serving local lines were vintage rakes of mainly non-corridor carriages (though some had a lavatory between two compartments) hauled by equally ancient though well-kept locomotives. The passing loops at stations on the North Devon line were too short to accommodate holiday trains, so points had to be clipped by hand and the last few coaches backed into sidings. Signalling, stations, coaches, locomotives: they were all inferior to the Great Western's, yet average speeds were usually higher. Only the main line to Exeter was of trunk standard, and even that lacked water troughs to enable the same locomotive to continue without delay. So engines had to be changed at Salisbury, the replacement being ready to leave within an incredible three minutes of the incoming machine having drawn its train to a halt.

No traffic opportunities were ignored. The great coup was persuading the White Star line to switch from Liverpool to Southampton. After the merger with Cunard, which was the government's condition for financing the *Queen Mary*, up to five trains ran for a single sailing. The Atlantic Coast Express for the West Country for most of the year included just single coaches for numerous destinations, yet on summer Saturdays it ran in up to six parts, each with a restaurant car. Hop pickers were carried cheap on Saturday mornings on trains normally used for taking workers to London. Sundays and Bank Holidays saw armies of excursionists going to the Kent resorts, still by steam.

Again, the remarkable thing is that virtually every word of this is equally true of both before and after the war that put the Southern in the front line and treated it harshly in just about every way. The story of its legendary wartime efforts, notably in making the 'victory' of Dunkirk possible by rapidly distributing the returning troops, does not belong here... but such a style and momentum had been created that return to peacetime normality was achieved quickly.

Naturally the war stopped electrification. But, in Britain's darkest hour, the Southern persuaded the government to approve the building of urgently-needed so-called mixed traffic engines (since express ones were not a wartime priority). Designed by Oliver Bulleid, the only Southern top manager at odds with the railway's overall cautious approach, the Merchant Navy and other new Pacific classes were the wonder of the age. And though some of Bulleid's more experimental efforts were expensive failures, the Merchant Navy, Battle of Britain and West Country classes meant that those areas not yet electrified saw heavier and faster trains... and a delightful Indian Summer of steam that we relished at the time and still talk of today.

The effect was particularly dramatic in the West Country, where the Southern's system west of Exeter, nicknamed the Withered Arm, came to life with the great increase in holidays with pay. Indeed, in the early days of the Western's dieselisation the steam-hauled Atlantic Coast Express regularly beat the Cornish Riviera Express to Exeter. Today many Weymouth and Bournemouth passengers would willingly swap their modern Wessex Electrics for the Bulleid locomotive-hauled trains of the fifties and well into the sixties, and Bournemouth along with Brighton laments the loss of its Pullman Belle.

Under the overall Southern style and unity, variety abounded. You could almost be sure to have the train on the grandly-named North Devon and Cornwall Junction Light Railway to yourself, but noted that the heavy clay traffic was taken to the railway's own river port of Fremington, while down in Cornwall clay was carried on the Wenford Bridge line by 2–4–0 Beattie tanks of mid-Victorian origin. Nothing could

beat the climb from Calstock in the Tamar Valley up to Callington as the ex-LSWR class 0–4–4 tank shrieked to announce itself at successive level crossings (this was another Light Railway). All this was a far cry from London where the Southern owned about half the large termini, or Folkestone Harbour where successive generations of overseas visitors' first travel in England was on a slow-moving train with several locomotives panting up the incline to the main line.

We never turned the Southern quite into the religion that the Great Western was, but admire and enjoy it undoubtedly we did. Above all it made such a pleasure of getting to the port to catch our first ship out of Britain. Boat trains were a way of life. They included the posh Golden Arrow Pullman and the Night Ferry on which you could sleep from Victoria to Paris and later Brussels. Even to see such a train set out on or finish its journey gave one a tingle.

Merchant Navy class Pacific No 21C13 Blue Funnel charges down the LSWR main line with the newly introduced Devon Belle Pullman train in 1947. In the foreground Drummond 700 class 0–6–0 No 699 is engaged in shunting duties probably at Weybridge goods depot whilst working Nine Elms duty No 70.

Bournemouth Belle

*Basingstoke was a favourite haunt of the artist from 1964
until the end of steam on the Southern in 1967. It was an
ideal location to watch expresses roaring through and lesser
trains at rest. For good measure, there was also an interesting
engine shed to browse around. The Bournemouth Belle was
the last steam-hauled Pullman car train to run in Britain and
was the domain of the magnificent Bullied Pacifics until they
were superseded by class 47 diesels. Rebuilt West Country No
34042* Dorchester *thunders through with the Waterloo-
bound 'Belle' whilst an unrebuilt sister engine No 34002*
Salisbury *makes a smoky start with an up stopping train.*

Waterloo Departure

During their latter years the Southern Railway's Schools class 4–4–0s were regular performers on the summer Saturdays trains from Waterloo to Lymington Pier for the Isle of Wight ferry. One of these sturdy engines No 30903 Charterhouse of Nine Elms shed stands in typical summer holiday weather at Waterloo station with one of these trains. The season is 1962. The last survivors of the class were withdrawn by the end of the year. The Lymington trains were their swansong. The Schools (or class V) were designed by R.E.L. Maunsel and introduced in 1930. They were, and remained, the most powerful 4–4–0 type ever built in Britain. The total of forty was built by 1935. All were named after well known public schools.

8
STATIONS

TODAY you have to go to India to see railway stations used as a meeting place of all humanity. The time was that you could enter a station and immerse yourself in a spectacle greater than most modern tourist attractions for free, or were it a 'closed' station for an old penny.

Nothing has changed as radically as railway stations, large and small; but here the nostalgia is in the major termini and junctions of childhood memory or our parents' descriptions and experiences passed down orally. Memories indeed... of noise, glamour, dirt, excitement, theatrical activity between lulls, a hundred and one sources of interest and fascination (and temptation to spend your money).

It is perhaps recalling the sounds and noises of yesteryear's great stations that most emphasises the change. For a start even most male youngsters went through a stage (female ones were less able to predict what was going to happen) of being scared of locomotives whose safety valves might suddenly explode into a deafening roar or whose whistles might make you think it were the day of judgement. Boys of three or four could be seen trying to tug their fathers away from the front end of the train. Aunts who passed by engines — like everything else trying to ignore the surroundings — would, if caught by a sudden blowing of the safety valve or whistle, complain their hearing would never be the same again. Sometimes their forecast was right, for delicate human ears were not meant for such strains, often amplified under low station roofs. Tinnitus sufferers would certainly have a ringing in their ears for weeks to come. It was not just train engines that upset the peace, but all those shunters adding and detaching vehicles, an especial danger being the sudden coming to life of one whose crew had previously seemed intent on spending eternity in a bay platform or on a through track maybe at the end of a scissors crossover.

Gongs rung by signalmen to inform station staff of a forthcoming movement could also make you jump. So, of course, could the unhitching of the brake pipe when a locomotive was being cut off; generations of passengers arriving at Liverpool Street knew that the line's Westinghouse brake was particularly violent in its undoing.

Other sounds were friendly, and how we miss some of them... the wheel tapper instantly getting to work as soon as a train halted, paper boys and refreshment vendors 'shouting' their wares hoping to bring customers to the window, porters and postmen uttering the destination of parcels and bags being sorted onto lined-up carts and trolleys, some of the parcels (such as dogs, cats, day-old chicks, calves) themselves adding to the cacophony. The noisy movement of barrows often interrupted conversation and prevented you hearing what the porters were shouting. (Until the opening of centralised creameries which led to the conveyance of liquid milk in most areas just before World War II, manhandled milk churns let out excruciating noises... and some could still be seen or more usually heard well into the 1950s.) Often bells could be heard ringing in signal cabins; the messages of the platform gongs were ever compulsive if you were not too close to be frightened, and you listened for the sound of point movements, and signals being raised or lowered. Even point rodding and signal wires contributed their bit. Then everything would be drowned by the sound of a hundred chattering passengers rapidly pacing along the platform.

Different stations of course had their own smells. The kind of locomotive and the coal being burnt made the largest impact, but odours from breweries or other industries might contribute, along with livestock and perishables on the platform. Southern waiting rooms like trains had their disinfectant smell almost as distinctive as the acrid smoke of LNER engines. Gentlemen had their hair cut in underground salons beside lavatories whose pong could be detected well above ground. Refreshment rooms could attract with their freshness and newly-baked morning goods, or smell like stale pubs, and the air in waiting rooms ranged from that of a respectable hotel drawing room to that of the doss house.

As for things to see and do, they were endless. Consider how much has been removed from a typical station. For starters, a rich variety of train indications, from finger-pointing boards inserted individually into the brackets for each train of the day at many stations to permanent enamel displays of departures that would cover an entire timetable. Roller blinds might display only half an hour of departures at peak times but the entire quieter night

The arrival side at Paddington probably in the early to mid-1950s—note the pre-war cab on the left and Jowett car to the right. The locomotive is Castle class 4–6–0 No 7006 Lydford Castle *allocated to Gloucester Horton Road so presumably the train is from Cheltenham.*

period and list every calling place and connection of every train. Woe betide if the porter responsible for moving them on failed to do so. Elsewhere a board with each train's details was manually put on display, at Glasgow Central in a huge exhibition of train details keeping three or four men constantly on the trot at busy times. Posters listing departures and platforms at large stations had a supplementary 'Today's Arrangements' pinned on. Infrequent travellers tended to ignore the lot and ask—and then ask again to ensure consistency of reply.

Departures were only one thing the railways told you about themselves. Booking halls and enquiry offices were as fascinating as public libraries, and which of us has not collected a handful of pamphlets about new services and excursions for entertainment while on the journey or waiting for our train in the refreshment room. They did not have to be about journeys we were actually likely to make ourselves, since they always revealed details of a region's social and economic activity. Remember, too, that you bought the railways' own magazines and items like their annual holiday guides from the booking office. Then there were the posters. Around a large station you could see displayed the latest work of many of the best commercial artists of the day, posters now rare and expensive collectors' pieces. For good measure the Great Western displayed relief maps (Dartmoor no doubt formed out of deep papier mâché) while the ex-North Eastern lines on the LNER had ceramic maps of the former system, somewhat lavatorial but at least easy to clean. Both types survived well into the 1960s; a few still do.

The ticket collector chalked up whether trains were on time (often just T) or how many minutes late. Glass case models of the latest locomotives were waiting for your penny for charity, their driving wheels whirling for half a minute when so fed… and, joy of joys, at many stations you could not only hear the bells in the signalboxes (and telephone conversations if windows were open in summer) but actually see track layouts and levers being pulled. Remember when a major station such as the Midland's Leicester would have signalboxes within sight of each other, and when signals and scissors crossovers mid-way down platforms were common?

Waiting rooms were not the favourites of young enthusiasts but could still be rewarding in their furnishings, fires and posters (and also their complements of human beings). Even two-platform stations at resorts like Torquay had separate first and third class and ladies' rooms, while larger junctions segregated their classes if not the sexes even in the refreshment rooms, and it was not only *Punch* that suggested that sandwiches were fresher in first. You were, of course, never expected to have to cross by bridge or subway to buy a cup of tea any more than to relieve yourself. Each platform or island was like a self-contained borough within a city, a focal point being the bookstall.

Bookstalls often seemed a geometric confusion: papers, placards, magazines and books dangling, hanging, projecting themselves at every conceivable angle to supplement the main horizontal and vertical displays with never a vacant inch. Trade was prodigious, railwaymen and daily passengers creating a base of regular business with chance sales to occasional passengers on top. Frequently you could find items at station bookstalls not stocked in the cities or towns the stations served—such as newspapers published at

distant points served by the station (between the London termini you could find every regional daily) as well as publications about the railways themselves. Thousands purchased their first railway magazine (and usually *The Railway Magazine*, the only popular periodical devoted to railways before 1939) with hard-earned pocket money as part of a station expedition.

If you could resist the temptations of the refreshment room, and never even considered the full-fledged restaurant for a three-course meal that most sizeable stations also supported, you still had to pass the automatic chocolate machines. For many this was not so difficult since Nestlé's chocolate, which somehow had a monopoly, was not generally regarded as the best. A penny might be better spent on engraving your name or message on a strip of aluminium. Is memory accurate in recalling that you were allowed twenty-six characters or spaces? A penny was also needed to get to the toilet (apart from the gents urinals)... an expensive luxury. But then if the station were closed, strictly speaking your platform ticket only purchased the right to be present for an hour, though only occasionally would a mean ticket collector make a surcharge. Where surcharges were common, you might get

Liverpool Street is an 18 platform terminus just within the City of London and is divided into two almost equal halves. The Norfolkman is seen at platform No 9 on the west side, with Stratford-based Britannia class 7 Pacific No 70001 Lord Hurcomb *providing the motive power, in the early 1950s. The Great Eastern section used discs rather than lamps to indicate train classification. There were some local codes, one of which is seen on the L1 2–6–4 tank on the left.*

Edinburgh Waverley platform 10 in the summer of 1961 with class A4 No 60024 Kingfisher *at the head of The Elizabethan— 9.30am Waverley to King's Cross. Waverley is a large rambling station of 21 platforms with a relatively low overall roof no more than 42ft above rail level due to the legal restriction of 'Servitudes'—the Scottish equivalent of 'Ancient Lights'. The station is now partially electrified for both East Coast and West Coast services.*

better value booking a journey to a neighbourhood station, one or two coppers enabling you to hop on to a train at most places when stations were packed tighter together. For the most part ticket collectors and porters welcomed your interest, and even the station inspector might guide you to the next point of interest as though he were a museum curator.

There were still many other things you could do: buy cards (and stamps from machines) and post them, platform letter boxes being cleared as frequently as any, telephone, buy an ice cream from a cart pushed up the platform… and of course help the old lady who had not immediately found a porter with her luggage, hoping to recoup the cost.

Porters were however usually in evidence. The biggest difference we would notice going back to a busy station of thirty or more years ago is not the trains themselves but the sheer pressure of people. Literally hundreds worked at larger junctions, not including those in the district offices through whose front doors staff were ever passing. Many big stations used to serve more routes than today; trains were often busier, waits longer—and it was much more common to be seen off or met by family or servants. You have to experience checking in at Heathrow on a bad day to remember what it was

like, and how much space luggage takes between waiting passengers. Remember when a smart porter would capture the luggage of half a dozen arriving or departing passengers, when mother would worry that the hat box balanced at the top of the pile would fall off and dad was ever counting, counting where everything was and then digging into his pocket for an appropriate tip?

Yet all this is like describing the stage set without the story or actors. While much life went on regardless of trains, there was never any doubt that it was really about arrivals and departures. Patterns were then quite different from today's. Preston, Taunton, York, Sheffield Midland, Perth... almost everywhere except in the South East, locals accounted for a high proportion of trains; expresses were infrequent and major affairs of great length (in number of carriages) and ceremony. The pattern was very familiar. After a siesta, a batch of local and branch trains would disgorge their passengers and parcels including produce of the countryside grown for city dwellers. While most passengers would surrender their tickets at the barrier, handfuls took advantage of the ingenious and often time-honoured connections to London or other distant cities. Often guard's vans were unloaded onto separate barrows for the main-line connection and local destinations and wheeled noisily away... having hardly got out of sight before a second two-coach train terminated at the same spot and other porters manoeuvred more barrows beside the opening van doors.

Everything came to life: booking hall, waiting and refreshment rooms, bookstalls, shunting engines. The engines took tail-end traffic (such as milk, gas tanks, and horse and cattle vehicles) off some of the local or branch trains and perhaps then attached themselves to a restaurant car to be added to the express. Steadily the main up platform, described by Arnold Bennett as the more modish, became crowded with passengers, railwaymen and luggage, the stationmaster in his silk hat emerging like an important second-line actor just after the gong had rung the requisite number of times and the home, starter and slotted distant arms of the semaphores had raised or lowered. Signals, like station furniture and the general state of well-being or decay, varied sharply according to railway and prosperity of the area.

Then the principal actor, the express: not just one of an hourly or bi-hourly pattern uniform with the others but an individual character with its own regular rolling stock and crew, and probably its antecedents deep in history if not running exactly to a time-honoured schedule. Whether or not officially named or nicknamed, each express had great personality, and its arrival—maybe fifteen coaches of it—justified the grandeur of the station. Ironically the frequency of services was much less at those great cathedrals of steam north of Birmingham than at the generally inferior stations (except London ones) in the South. Even most long-distance arrivals at Birmingham were real events (New Street and Snow Hill being as different as any two could be) while over at Leicester, an Anglo-Scottish express had onlookers as fascinated as the audience of any theatrical production.

Much had to be done in the few minutes expresses were halted. Passengers had to find their reserved seats, and even if not reserved would have to ensure they were in the right coach or portion of those trains going to various destinations. Men seeing their womenfolk off would try to select a compartment with 'appropriate' travelling companions. Those who wanted their own company looked for empty compartments at the front or back. Those disliking long walks through the corridor settled for a carriage near the restaurant car.

Major stops usually saw the restaurant car between meal sittings, and a red flag would go out to indicate that supplies were being taken on board. Such stops often brought a change of locomotive. A shunting engine might be attaching or detaching at the back, while porters and postmen struggled with barrow loads against the clock. A minute before departure it might seem that the train would never be ready but, encouraged by the inspector's whistle, miraculously a couple of dozen doors closed within a few seconds, the last to be held open perhaps being for a passenger who had shot off to the refreshment room for sustenance. We forget that buffet cars were rare even in the last great days of steam, the on-board choice being between a full meal (including perhaps a set coffee service) or nothing. If you did not take your seat in the restaurant car, you took your own refreshments or fled to a platform refreshment room, the knowledgeable jumping off from the nearest door. Those in charge of platform trolleys were also strategically placed to start business but often lacked time to serve the entire train.

Excitement was enhanced by several factors. Not only were there few expresses but many were the only service on its route or of its kind during the entire day. The next stop was often hours away; London itself having a vast range of places reached non-stop. To be on board you were really someone on a true adventure. Destination boards added to the glamour.

Longer non-stop runs meant occasional 'runners' rushing through. Exeter St David's, for example, had just as keen an atmosphere whether the Torbay Express was arriving non-stop from Paddington or the summer Cornish Riviera Limited was cleared for a full-speed run through the centre road. Throughout the land, when things went with the usual precision, tension rose as the last goods or local or shunting engine was tucked safely in the loop, bay or platform. The stop and distant signals cleared in quick succession, followed it seemed only moments later by the whistle of the express telling all to stand clear. At many locations, including Exeter St David's, level crossing gates had to be closed but pedestrians were allowed across only seconds ahead of the racing train. At Grantham, Doncaster, wherever, there would always be a huddle of onlookers to wonder in awe at the organisation that allowed the Flying Scotsman or the pre-war Silver Jubilee to pass uninterrupted on its exalted way... though of course a hot box on a preceding goods or even a parcel trolley falling off the platform did occasionally cause delay.

Precision timing: exhilaratingly, it happened day by day, week by week, much of the quieter time of the year. It has always mainly been passengers who delay trains, in steam days especially crowds often affecting locomotive performance by their extra weight as well as necessitating longer station stops. One reason why things more usually ran like clockwork is precisely that most of the nation's fastest trains had very limited stops. On some lines, but especially Great Western ones, the rule has always been the fewer the stops the better the punctuality, today's more frequent stops no doubt attracting extra traffic but inevitably affecting performance at busy times.

Birmingham Snow Hill was a much more salubrious station than New Street having been rebuilt c1914. Modified Hall class 4–6–0 No 6991 Acton Burnell Hall *is seen at platforms 7 and 8 with a relief portion of the Pines Express, reporting number 1O39, on 7 August 1965. The main train was diesel hauled by a class 47. No 6991 lasted to the end of Western Region steam working and was withdrawn in December 1965 from Oxford shed.*

70

Some railwaymen who cared that their passengers (never then 'customers') enjoyed the best used the word tragedy to explain the fact that most people who went by train could not realise how good the service normally was. They went on excursions for which other trains were not so readily swept out of the way, on summer Saturdays—when increasingly overwhelming pressure inevitably meant longer and less comfortable journeys, even though through trains and carriage options were increased.

While again it is sad that much of the population only experienced stations and trains when they were under unreasonable pressure (some indeed only went by train during the war), the days when quarts had to be fitted into pint pots produced their own comradeship and fascination. The main platforms at major stations were seldom vacant, another train being allowed in cautiously as the first left at many places. Those hoping to get a cup of tea formed veritable rugby scrums in refreshment rooms whose overworked staff might only get round to collecting abandoned cups when no clean ones were left. In the days before plastic and paper, many cups were taken onto trains, and at desperate times the youngest member of staff would be sent to scour compartments and corridors during station stops.

At night you had a job to find an inch of bench in waiting rooms not covered by those pretending to be if not actually asleep. That was especially true of Crewe which became a wartime joke as a result of comedians and musicians frequently being held up there changing to and from Bangor where the BBC's variety department was evacuated. Wise souls not only knew all the station nooks and crannies but what might be better facilities in the surrounding area. Many pubs indeed flourished on late running, and had to look for new custom when the railways ceased carrying crowds on late-running services.

Never again will platforms even at today's busier stations see such crowds and paraphernalia spread out along their entire lengths, or such pedestrian congestion at their approaches. 'Queue here to walk', said a jocular visitor struggling to get his family to the station at the end of their holiday. But then we forget how the normal rhythm of stations could also be interrupted by some seasonal or special event. For generations, everyone attending a distant sporting event did so by train, raising the roof with their singing and chanting. Politicians and trade union organisers invariably came and went through the station door along with their supporters, determined to make an occasion of the arrival or departure. Sunday school outings and other school parties (indeed large proportions of whole schools on a daily basis in many places) made their distinctive noises. Many times a year a typical busy station platform sounded like a jovial beach in high summer: laughter, giggling and even good-natured shrieking building into perpetual crescendos. Special parties were often let in or out by side doors or gates specially unlocked for them.

Though such parties were very much part of the scene, and watching them and how they were marshalled along could be entertaining in itself, the young enthusiast sometimes wished they could hurry away... their boisterousness interrupting concentration and preventing you from hearing the signalbox bells.

Today's travellers, used to greater comfort, would never suffer the delays

and overcrowding of yesteryear yet often think fondly of their own or their parents' memories when getting there was half the fun. Indeed, even on the most congested summer Saturdays in the late 1940s and 1950s, people frequently spoke of the journey as being the best part of the holiday. They had never before seen such a kaleidoscope of scenery and human and farming activity as a long-distance railway journey made available. Children who have not experienced all human life in a railway station have especially missed out. We even enjoyed many delays… especially those to local trains on peak summer Saturdays when everything might run two hours late including the departure of an all-stations-and-halts branch train from a bay not allowed out onto the main line until its appropriate slot between expresses. Less fun was being stuck in a non-corridor coach at a junction for an hour or more waiting for a spare platform. Now we see under-used if not abandoned platforms everywhere, but once it was platform rather than track capacity that was the limiting factor. Even on the generally well-regulated Great Western and its successor the Western Region, queuing to get into Paddington or Bristol Temple Meads might add twenty-five percent even to a long journey.

Strangely, in some areas a higher proportion of people occasionally use a station today than ever before. That is because more of us sometimes go to distant cities or their airports, notably London, and the train's specialist role is appreciated. But they mainly arrive in their own cars rather than on foot or by bus (or tram), and they lack yesteryear's mixture of excitement and apprehension. It would not occur to them that once the character of a town or city might be judged by its railway station.

LNER class D49/2 4–4–0 No 62751 The Albrighton *stands in platform 8 at York station with a train from the Scarborough line, whilst a V2 class 2–6–2 waits at the signal on the down through road c1954. There is a carriage and wagon examiner checking the carriages adjacent to the V2. The layout of York station is now considerably altered following electrification and the removal of the through roads.*

9
VILLAGE STOP

THE locomotive work had been exemplary. Though from the timetable it might have seemed a very secondary train, the streamlined West Country class Pacific had six well-used passenger and five parcels vehicles behind it. Departure from the junction was late, and driver and fireman were obviously intent on making up time. The uphill running was vigorous, the exhaust having a regular rhythm like the sound of a factory driven by water power.

Over the summit, and now the enginemen will surely have their reward. But as speed tops seventy a couple of miles on, the brakes are slammed on, and despite a long, plaintive whistle we are brought almost to a stand at the home signal and drift at walking speed through a deserted platform and beyond to the starter.

Silence. That is to say silence from the train, but gradually we take in the surroundings. On one side cattle are being driven along the lane for their evening milking, and close by on the other there is another lane leading to a field where a village fair is being held. We just catch the sound of the band, and decide to walk forward, our footsteps making almost everybody sitting in the compartments look toward the corridor before we are actually seen.

The guard has his van in the back of the front coach. 'Cattle on the line and the express delayed in front,' he tells us. We open the window of the very front door and are almost in the middle of the fair—or is it a village show. Almost at once the brass band comes to a stop, the musicians pack up their music, music stands and instruments and bundle themselves into a couple of shooting brakes, dashing off no doubt for an evening engagement.

Leisurely returning from the signalbox, the fireman informs his mate it is going to be some time yet. The driver alights with oil can, but perhaps more out of habit than necessity for no oiling is actually done. Maybe he just wants fresh air... but he quickly turns his attention to a couple of men standing near the fence. Escaping steam makes just sufficient hiss to prevent our catching the conversation. The refreshment tent has now been closed. Most people have drifted away. The village clock chimes six.

We walk back a couple of carriages and look out again. Making her way toward the lane, at the very end of the field immediately beneath the door, is a tall country girl in her late teens with bright cheeks, milky legs and arms and thick, dark hair which falls on either side of her head as she raises her hazel eyes and we say 'Good evening'.

Cautiously starting with pleasantries about the weather, the conversation turns to what kind of village this is and we discover she used to catch the train to school since the local one had been closed, though there are still two shops. One of the men who have been talking with the driver hears this and adds 'And three pubs'. Pausing momentarily on his way home, he lightheartedly warns: 'Now, don't be getting into trouble with fancy up-country folk, Betty'.

The smallest hint of a blush crosses her forehead and for a moment she seems to examine her shoes. Our own shoes being three feet above the level of her head, there is fat chance of 'getting into trouble'. Before we know if we are going to continue talking, the guard passes through the train. 'Sorry for the delay; we'll be away in a couple of minutes now.'

That frees our tongues. Names are formally exchanged. She likes riding horses and has her own pony. She got a prize at the village show... yes, it was the show with a bit of gymkhana in the field behind, but it was mainly over by tea time, though there is going to be a dance in the village hall.

'Are you going?'

'Nobody to go with. Nobody I want to, anyway.'

Now, there's a challenge. 'What time does it start?' Indeed, what time is there a train back, and how might we explain our non-appearance down the line. What might a taxi cost?

The reader will, of course, have guessed it. A rustling of a wire by the ballast tells that the signal has been pulled. Up she goes. We had not noticed the driver climbing back on board. In an instant she whistles and the wheels are turning, not even a fraction of a slip. Well, it is down hill.

'Nice talking,' she says.

'See you—soon!'—but it is too late to add more, whatever that might have been.

We will never know if she prepared herself for the dance, or turned up and was taken over by someone else, or whether she had children... or whether she ever thinks back to that lineside encounter.

Like girls in pigtails allegedly one-minded about ponies, we were supposed only to think of the diameter of driving wheels and cut-offs. Yet making the best of railways was a total experience and that meant at least acknowledging the existence of the opposite sex. What happened to the geography student going home to her colliery village from Swansea university to swot for finals? Or the girl on her way to Newquay who wanted to appreciate the moonlit Exe estuary from the corridor but spoilt things by revealing she worked for BR at Shrewsbury and hated their guts?

Most respectable young ladies of course did not look for compartments by themselves. Even restaurant car stewards seldom put both sexes together, though occasionally you might be in luck (if seriously out of pocket).

Once we had our regular girl friend, the joys of the non-corridor compartment of an uncrowded train were much to be savoured. Indeed, in the days when parents stayed at home, and home meant everyone in the same living room, where else could you enjoy upholstered privacy better than in the spacious compartment of a non-corridor train making only brief stops at deserted stations and halts? It was certainly better than going to the cinema... and that apart from the fact that, however passionate, you were still a railway lover. When worldly progression meant going by car, kissing stops were naturally lay-bys from which (without seeming to go off the boil) you could see the passage of the day's best express, perhaps double headed just having ascended a major incline.

Railways never were divorced from life.

10
LONDON MIDLAND

SHORTLY after one dirty tank engine shunts the last of the coal trucks clear of the platform, another unceremoniously arrives with a train of three non-corridor carriages. A few doors open, passengers alight and those waiting to join shuffle up and down the platform peering in to discover the least undesirable companions for the ride into town. Unable to see through the filthy windows, a couple of people open doors to establish what room there is inside. In first class a gentleman brushes the seat with his hands and places a newspaper on it before sitting, while next door two schoolboys swing their satchels onto the moquette and raise a miniature dust storm. The driver looks back waiting for the guard's signal; a curious passenger has noticed his engine is fifty years old and its paintwork so covered in grime that its number has been chalked up to make identification easier.

As the stopping train eases out, pouring sulphur into the air, this passenger looks around and notices that the station itself could do with a coat of paint rather than just a wash. Here is a place that nobody seems much to love; only the edge of the platform has ever been swept clean. Only a handful of the railway's own posters add a touch of brightness…

A typical London Midland Region express The Mancunian had a pedigree, if not a nomenclature, stretching back to the days of the old 'Premier Line'. A Camden-based rebuilt Scot No 46162 Queen's Westminster Rifleman *climbs out of Euston with the 6.00pm Euston–Manchester in the early 1950s. The stock is the very comfortable LMS period III coaches built from 1933 onwards, although the leading vehicle is of BR build, distinguished by the circular toilet window.*

An Anglo-Scottish express, the 11.15am Birmingham to Glasgow, ascends Beattock, without the aid of a banking engine, hauled by class 8P 4–6–2 No 46203 Princess Margaret Rose *in August 1952. All the coaches are painted in the first BR standard livery of crimson-and-cream. The locomotive is now preserved and based at the Midland Railway Centre at Butterley.*

inviting you to travel in luxury to far-away exotic places such as Llandudno, Buxton and the Clyde Coast. As a few more workers, school children and a couple of women with prams arrive for the next train, nobody daring to sit on the dust-laden seats, a whistle sounds and an express runs through the opposite platform. Hauled by a large, smart red Royal Scot class locomotive, it has eight or nine carriages including a well-filled restaurant car through whose windows you can see clearly. The destination boards displaying the train's route on the roof of the carriages momentarily evoke thoughts of distant relatives or reports of sporting events, but few of the passengers waiting to go into town have ever visited the places named or have any expectation of doing so during their lives.

The scene might have been at dozens of stations in England, Wales or Scotland immediately before World War II, or for that matter in the late 1940s. The LMS was a railway of contrasts: a veneer of respectability over an infrastructure of neglect; some of the world's best expresses and innumerable locals of unimaginable dirt; the best-kept main-line tracks in

the world and hundreds of stations whose neglect was beyond redemption.

The largest of the Big Four of the Grouping era, it was also the largest transport organisation in the entire world, the largest commercial organisation of any kind in the British Empire. Much of it was unbelievably humdrum, yet much of it had great glamour. When Henry Hall the band leader was wooed by the BBC, he took a salary drop of fifty percent from what the LMS was paying him as their principal band leader, normally based at Gleneagles. And if this seems surprising, it should be added that among the list of its 'biggests', the LMS ran the largest hotel chain in the Empire, regulating the top social life in many of Britain's most important cities as well as setting new standards of elegance from Stratford-upon-Avon to the Scottish Highlands. It also had a huge shipping fleet and was involved in every kind of industrial development.

'LMS: Hell of a mess,' schoolboys loyal to the other railways used to yell, yet it was the LMS traffic receipts that gave a quicker guide to the state of the nation's trade than any other single set of figures. In many ways it not only served great slices of Britain—from the mouth of the Thames and South Wales through the great industrial heartlands of the Midlands, North and Scottish Lowlands to the coastal extremities of Holyhead and Wick—but it *was* Britain. It had an importance hard to comprehend in

today's motor and air age, and management problems that perhaps set the trend for loss of pride in the job that Britain has so dearly paid the price for in the competitive commercial world.

The railway was forged out of the compulsory merger of numerous companies of great individuality and different tradition. Though some of the others, such as the Lancashire & Yorkshire, were themselves very substantial affairs, in England the main pair were the London & North Western and the Midland, ever arch rivals. The LNWR advertised itself as the Premier Line and its main West Coast route out of Euston to the Midlands, North Wales, Manchester, Liverpool, Blackpool, the Lake District and Carlisle had a quality second to none. Autocratic, gentlemanly, placing equal importance on track, locomotives and carriages, it pioneered many world standards.

The Midland, out of St Pancras but governed from Derby, was a much tougher affair run by stiff businessmen, with some of the best carriages anywhere in the world but relying on small locomotives that whisked passengers in short, feather-weight trains... and of course earned its fortune carrying coal, by queues of daily trains to London.

There was no way the pair would work happily together, and it is interesting to recall that for a moment before Grouping the government toyed with having six rather than four companies, giving Scotland one to itself and making another out of the Midland

From 1958 to 1967 the West Coast main line between Manchester, Liverpool and Birmingham to Euston suffered much disruption due to the electrification and rebuilding of stations. This is Coventry station c1961 in a state of confusion with very few amenities for passengers. Two Stanier class 3P 2–6–2Ts are visible both apparently doing a 'House of Peers' (nothing in particular but doing it very well). Further along the down platform there is a two-car Metro-Cammell DMU.

and Great Central. But while it was felt right to force mergers and generally control the railways more effectively, since they wielded tremendous power, the ethos was that as well as being competitive they also had to be profitable, and it was feared that Scotland might not adequately support its own system.

As an example of the problems of forced marriage, the Midland men who immediately came out on top insisted that their view of locomotive policy was correct... insisted that since their own expresses were frequently double headed, those running out of Euston should be given a second engine. Stories went the rounds of North Western drivers being brought to tears when told they needed a second engine to do work that one had happily done before. Such arguments were coupled with changed promotion prospects for many and the loss of the much-loved individual liveries. While Midland red was adopted for express engines (and all carriages) lesser locomotives went black, and that alone killed much pride.

With a quarter of a million employees, over four hundred different classes of locomotive, three thousand goods stations scattered over a system of over 7,000 route miles in Ulster as well as England, Wales and Scotland, and major involvement in every region other than England's North East, the LMS was clearly going to be an administrative nightmare. Not even in the United States had anyone at that time faced such a management challenge.

It began badly, with internal squabbles, lack of guidelines and industrial troubles. Profitability started poorly and became steadily worse with strikes, depression, road competition and an inflexible government. Yet there were solid achievements, especially in paving the way for today's InterCity services.

In some ways the LMS never got it together, and arguably the decision to centralise management was the first and principal mistake. But it was at least partly rescued and energetically led by one of the most famous of all twentieth-century railmen, and also one of the least likely: Lord Stamp (as he later became), teetotaller, Nonconformist lay preacher,

This is a pure LMS train on the ex-Midland line out of Leeds in early BR days; the route was a London Midland Region penetrating line, which was later transferred to the North Eastern Region. BR-built class 5 4–6–0 No 44667 of Derby shed passes Holbeck Low Level with an ordinary passenger train for either Bradford or Morecambe formed of LMS corridor coaches.

writer of economics text books and company director via the ranks of the Inland Revenue. Astonishment at his appointment was increased by the fact that he was President (following the American example) though soon also became chairman and had the distinction of reporting to himself as he wielded huge, decisive power. Perhaps the prototype of eighties-style bosses, he paid himself well. When a shareholder questioned his £15,000, he retorted that it equalled a ham sandwich for each shareholder and 'I'm sure that you will not begrudge me my ham sandwich'.

Lingering power struggles subsided as Stamp made Euston the undisputed base: the old Euston of Gothic portico and lodge (through which our taxi used to enter) of cathedral-like Great Hall and separate arrival and departure stations. Standardisation was Stamp's watchword. There was little time for niceties; it was standardisation by blunt hammer, a sinister dress rehearsal for nationalisation, though undoubtedly Stamp would have been a better leader of BR than any that were available.

The particular achievement was on the locomotive side. In the early years there was a desperate shortage of power as well as extravagant variety of type. The turning point came when William Stanier (later Sir William) was poached from the GWR and produced successive classes combining economy with power, as well as giving the LMS a distinctive touch. By 1938 Stamp was able to boast that standardisation and increase in power had resulted in the number of

locomotives being cut from 10,396 to 7,688 and more importantly the number of classes from 404 to 162. A huge slice of the spending went on engines and their fuel (the LMS reckoned that its six and a half million tons of coal burned annually gave employment to 26,500 miners) and that performance was totally dependent on steaming at the 'front end'.

Even the Royal Scots of the late 1920s had been largely designed by an outside company, but Stanier made the LMS self-sufficient, the Empire's largest engineering capacity under single ownership at his command. New classes followed rapidly in the 1930s, and expresses were speeded up as they became heavier and gave greater comfort. The crowning success was the streamlined Coronation Scot linking Euston with Glasgow... in the days when only two daytime expresses offered passengers a ride at ordinary fares. While the LMS greatly increased inter-city travel it was from a low base, and throughout its existence people from the provinces were far more likely to visit London aboard a sporting or military special.

Facilities were also improved at locomotive depots. Anything grander simply could not be afforded as the railway struggled with declining receipts. Electric traction was confined to a few isolated routes, no

Johnson class 1P 0–4–4 tank No 58047 leaves Wells (Priory Road) for Glastonbury & Street with a pull-and-push service in 1951. The S&D branch closed in October of that year. The small Somerset city of Wells was for a short period in the 1870s served by three separate companies, each with its own terminus. The main S&D system closed in March 1966.

major stations were built or even modernised, and the accident record was poor. The hotels and catering side employing 8,000 people invoked even higher standards; passenger comfort was increased even on most local services (in terms of quality of ride and space between seats as opposed to cleanliness). The LMS is fondly remembered for grand trains and hotels and its art, but slowly most stations deteriorated until even those around London's suburbs were unbelievably shabby. And the basic geography remained unchanged. The LMS ran three of the four routes across the Pennines and had many penetrating lines. It was like an octopus, with penetrating lines to Southend-on-Sea and Carmarthen, to mention but two.

Had the trade revival in the last pre-war years continued, the LMS might conceivably have made good. But coal and staff shortages, enormous extra traffic demands and the death of Lord Stamp in a London air raid in 1941 meant that at nationalisation

Ashchurch on the Midland's Bristol line still displays plenty of pre-Grouping influence in this September 1952 view. In the goods yard a Johnson 0–4–4T No 58071 is shunting cattle wagons. On the main line an LMS-built, right-hand drive class 4F 0–6–0 No 44123 in early BR livery heads a freight train south. The second wagon is lettered 'Glyncorrwg wgns'. Note the bracket signals, one purely Midland the other an upper quadrant replacement.

the country inherited a poor train set covering many key areas.

The London Midland was perhaps the least loved of all the Regions. It began by basically taking over the English and Welsh part of the LMS but was subject to many boundary changes. Nationalisation made relatively little difference, for many LMS practices were initially adopted nation-wide but there was no strong identification or tradition to be lost. As Harrow & Wealdstone quickly showed, the system remained accident prone, and punctuality and cleanliness were never remarkable. Though the LMR might take you to some of the most splendid scenery in North Wales, the Peak District and Lake District, some of its branch line trains were positively sordid. Many returning from Blackpool on excursion trains delayed by congestion at Preston or beyond cursed the fact that the Region delighted in making the most of its extensive stock of non-corridor trains. The Region seemed especially lacking in willpower to fight road competition in rural areas. Alone, it disallowed unstaffed halts, vigorously defending its policy that if traffic did not warrant the retention of staff then stations should close completely... as they sometimes did while being repainted or just accepting delivery of new seats or heating apparatus. Territory that had formerly been Midland seemed to avoid the worst of such depths, travel out of St Pancras definitely being superior to that from Euston. So late and overcrowded were many trains from Rugby that its folk generally abandoned the Euston route for Marylebone despite it offering much less choice of trains.

It was nonetheless the expresses that redeemed the Region. While few of us would have London Midland locals high up on our love list, the growing network of expresses was built on the firm LMS foundations of power, speed and comfort. The Premier Line (LNWR) had boasted the best track in the world north from Euston; that the London Midland certainly did not offer, had not maintained or rather restored after the war, but there was an attractive matter-of-factness in its generous and ever-increasing provision of fast trains. On many routes they seemed to come as frequently as suburban electrics at a time when you might spend 45 minutes beside the East Coast main line and see none.

It is thus not surprising that our London Midland images are mainly of powerful Pacifics hauling a dozen or more coaches. We of course especially remember them repainted in LMS maroon after the first BR red-and-cream livery in scenic settings such as the Lune Gorge before motorway days and Shap… and have a special place in our heart for the St Pancras to Scotland trains' passage of the Long Drag, the Settle & Carlisle. Sometimes, however, we revelled in the sheer ugliness of industrial areas through which the expresses swept like a breath of fresh air, and wondered how man could have contrived to produce

such miserable settings as many of the Lancashire ones on former Lancashire & Yorkshire territory. But we also fondly remember the expresses arriving at and leaving the great junction stations, especially Crewe, with a sense of occasion and hubbub on the platform with which today's travellers are not familiar. Now you have to go to a busy market to get the same kind of feel. How they got those giant expresses of ten carriages carrying six or more hundred souls away with such little delay, and how promptly the station inspector's signal was responded to by guard and driver, had one in wondering awe.

The LMS introduced the concept of InterCity services and also those much hated words 'organise' and 'reorganise'. It was, of course, not far into nationalisation that the whole West Coast main line was thrown into turmoil with electrification and rebuilding especially at Euston and Birmingham New Street. We were perhaps more proud of rather than in love with the country's first long-distance electrics, but did undoubtedly enjoy the enhanced role the Midland route from St Pancras played during the transition, even though the much-promoted Midland Pullman to Manchester was an early diesel set, precursor of the 125s.

The crews of two class 3F 0–6–0 tanks Nos 47276 and 47502 enjoy a lively chat as they descend the Lickey immediately behind a freight train, under permissive block regulations, to save time whilst working Bromsgrove banking duty No 6.

11
SPRING

WITH eager expectation each year, railwaymen welcome lengthening days both for the easier working conditions they bring and the extra traffic on offer. Now above all other times we realise how much we are governed by the seasons. Kids not allowed to walk home alone through the lanes after dark are now free to use the last train from town. The carriage of cement and other building materials increases dramatically and hardly a branch line fails to see its freight traffic grow until an accumulation of trucks left behind means a special train. Fertilisers are especially big business, sometimes involving a through train from the factory to branch line.

The grass embankments, neatly cut and burnt last year, are a picture with the spring flowers, and in their spare time (which at country stations often includes an hour or more between trains) railwaymen start tending their trackside allotments, ever watchful of each other's progress. Not only is the performance of each farmer noted by drivers, firemen and guards who pass up and down regularly, but often they deliver the latest pieces of farming technology ready for the coming season. But as the grass becomes greener, milk travels less far to London and other big cities. When there is a surplus, it is the milk furthest away that is turned into butter and cheese.

By the official beginning of spring the Cornish broccoli traffic (often fifty trainloads a day) might already be passed its peak. Daffodils from the Isles of Scilly, anemones and violets from South Devon, and soon early potatoes from the Spanish islands get the harvest cycle for another year truly under way. Oranges, lemons, grapefruit and bananas come in the ports year round, and banana specials from Avonmouth now reach their peak. More exotic fruit imports lie in the future, and even in winter and spring Britain grows most of its own flowers, many under glass especially in the Lea Valley just

A newly overhauled Hawksworth County class 4–6–0 No 1004 County of Somerset *approaches Thingley Junction with the 5.15pm Swindon to Bristol train in May 1953. The leading coach, No W2419W is a 'concertina' corridor third dating from 1906. During the early BR period it was fairly common to find a once grand pre-Grouping coach either in an ordinary passenger train or used as a strengthener in an express formation, more often than not situated right behind the locomotive.*

Stanier class 5 4–6–0 No 44876 takes water at Rowington troughs, between Hatton and Lapworth, as it heads a northbound express (reporting No 1M60) from Weymouth on 31 July 1965. The construction of the M40 has completely altered this view, removing the right-hand side of the cutting.

east of London, though nowhere are you surprised to see boxes of flowers for London or other cities being carefully transferred from station trolley to guard's van.

On the passenger side, much depends on the date of Easter. If it is late, winter imperceptibly changes into spring with only a gently increased traffic tempo. If it is early, bustle starts sooner... but then there is a relapse into virtual winter in the long weeks before Whitsun marks the beginning of the real buzz. Children and their Passengers' Luggage in Advance come back for the holiday and return to school. Some stationmasters have noticed a worrying tendency of parents taking the kids by car, but at least the trunks remain loyal to rail.

Expectation is surely in the air. The ports are busier, more people are travelling, painting gangs are at work smartening up this year's allocated stations and at the seaside many boarding houses are also sporting a new coat of paint to welcome the visitors the railway will eventually bring. A few indeed take advantage of special fares to pay an advance trip to their chosen resort and pick their boarding house, even the precise bedroom.

But then the wind veers east and it seems as though winter will never truly end. Only the final stages of the football season and other sporting events can be counted on dramatically to increase the number of passengers, specials sometimes taking more than ordinary timetable trains. Which teams are playing and where greatly influences the traffic planners, who thoroughly exploit local Derbys and think nothing of providing a day excursion to a city 250 miles away for cup matches (especially those resulting from unlikely wins). Many from Scotland and the North still pay their first visit to London for football. Sporting traffic is of major proportions and spring fixtures are far less frequently cancelled because of bad weather than winter ones.

All humanity goes to the races… but often by different trains. Gracious first class specials with hand-picked restaurant cars and crews naturally leave from the best platforms at the best times and have priority on the way, yet those tightly packed into third class non-corridor coaches are just as happy and certainly more demonstrative, betting now being on cards. Every ticket counts. The excursion offices carefully compare one season's races with another.

Revenue earning for some new carriages starts on race specials. The release of new stock from the carriage works reaches its seasonal peak. Some are sent to the furthest end of the system by parcels trains or added to the front of expresses to travel empty. But even if a new coach is in the middle of a revenue-earning train its immaculate condition stands out, for in the days of steam white roofs do not remain pure white for long.

Locomotive works are hurrying completion of the machines needed to operate the augmented summer services, spring being the favourite time for replacing aged pre-Grouping locomotives with more powerful contemporary ones. Each year sees 4–6–0s taking over the main burden on more routes, especially in the eastern counties of England and Scotland and in the Midlands where they have so far been less common.

Work on the track is also at a peak, causing many speed restrictions and weekend diversions… a necessary price to pay for higher speed limits introduced somewhere each year. The usual fierce arguments range (telephones often flung down) between the district traffic and engineering superintendents—the former determined to keep inconvenience to the public to a minimum and the latter to get on with the job with the least interruption from things like trains. Except over Easter and Whitsun weekends, when the engineers themselves take a holiday and just about every express arrives at every major station ridiculously early, Sunday travel is purgatory with little effort to clear tracks for those returning to cities in the evening. Those going back to London in readiness for Monday's work, if they cannot afford an overnight sleeper, are generally relegated to the worst rolling stock, usually every seat taken. The weight/power ratio is often diabolical, even minor gradients seeming like Everest. Arrivals at Euston, King's Cross and Paddington can be hours late.

Sunday evening trains back to town were distinctly not the ones we loved and were often in great contrast to the speedy Friday evening runs to the country. 'Since the last train is always so packed and late, I send my daughter on the one before,' said one father. And he was a district head, and the previous train was two and a half hours earlier. The suggestion there might be two 'last' Sunday trains was regarded as faintly silly. So where possible, weekends meant taking Monday off. Then we could treat ourselves to the very best train back and even take a detour in style.

Engineering work included refurbishing water troughs. Those at Church Lawford near Brandon & Wolston took ten weeks to do, the work only being done on Sundays, when Euston–Birmingham trains were diverted via Marton and Leamington, of course to the delight of some enthusiasts but

horror of those only using the railway to get to the other end. Even on week-days when the normal route was taken, having to stop at Rugby or Coventry to take water added a quarter of an hour to schedules. Even water towers needed a spring clean and out in the country drivers and signalmen had to regulate things so that no engine was caught short between open towers.

Diversions could also be caused by flooding, frequently brought about by a combination of snow melting on higher ground and heavy rain, and hardly a spring passed without the sea being whipped into ballast-removing fury if not causing a breach of a sea wall in South Devon or along the Cambrian Coast. But most floods were moderate, adding to the enjoyment of a journey along the valley. To those of us lucky enough to make such a trip it seems like only yesterday our spring train followed the Severn, Wye or Exe. The trees were still in bud, not blocking out the view of the river now burbling, now gushing, twigs caught on the lower branches showing how much higher the water recently reached. The joy of such journeys was that usually we were the only strangers, all other occupants (perhaps a dozen in an auto car) revelling in their familiarity with every detail yet amazed that the river was doing that, and remarking that the wild daffodils were out early or farmer so-and-so had not yet ploughed his biggest field. Those journeys were ones we never wished to end... and in truth they often lasted a long time including interminable waits at crossing stations and to take water. Predictably the guard was tall and very much in command.

Bank Holiday excursions and specials were a feature of both the spring and summer seasons. Class 5 2–6–0 No 42783 approaches Bewdley with a Rugeley to Stourport half-day excursion in August 1960. The train, consisting of ten non-corridor coaches, will reverse at Bewdley to reach Stourport. A 5101 class 2–6–2T awaits the road in the adjacent platform.

12
JOINT VENTURES

IN the 1950s Oliver Veltom was district superintendent at Shrewsbury, one of the old brigade, a gentleman, a railwayman through and through and a man who never forgot his friends or, for that matter, those who crossed him. He presided over one of the most delightful and intimate sections of railway there was and, as a Great Western officer among Great Western men, he was (usually) a form of benevolent God. His staff, some of whom could well remember true Cambrian Railway times and indeed the Abermule disaster (when two trains greeted each other head on in a cornfield meet on the single line), were once part of a particularly British institution, a Joint Railway with Salop as its headquarters. Outward and visible signs of this were the beckoning in and out of trains by lower quadrant signals put in place, originally, by the GWR and LNWR.

Veltom's remit covered the old LNW/GW, later LMS/GW line out to Buttington with running powers over Cambrian to Welshpool. But there were others running out of Shrewsbury, namely the road to Hereford, which was LNW/GW, and that from Chester to Birkenhead which involved him dealing as directly with both Euston and Paddington, even down to its parcels labels—a tale which Veltom could tell with some gusto. It relates to the Birkenhead end when the McNaught family had both presence and *presence* being clerk and stationmaster respectively.

Being at the far north-west end of a Great Western main line linked together with a powerful neighbour and partial rival, Birkenhead had to show an outward impartiality in both pre- and post-Grouping days. An example of this was the parcels office when care had to be taken to ensure fairness in despatch. A special calendar was pinned on to the wall adjacent to the counter, its pages carefully printed in two colours, black and red. On black days outgoing parcels for a destination served by both companies, say Birmingham, were stamped from a roll of non-adhesive Great Western tags involving the use of a messy gum brush, while on red days it was a neat perforated stamp from a Post Office style folder with lickable, quite tasty gum from Euston.

There was a time when father McNaught was stationmaster at Birkenhead and he spotted two separate gentlemen going round *his* station with a tape measure looking at and measuring up the advertising space. They turned out to be from the Publicity Departments at Euston and Paddington respectively, each one's objective to see that *his* company was getting its fair share. The stationmaster tactfully invited them both to lunch in the first-class refreshment room and put forward his own ideas for ultimate benefit.

The stationmaster at Birkenhead Woodside had the silvered buttons of Euston on his uniform while that important official at Salop sported the gold

Shrewsbury station in the late 1950s sees ex-GWR Hall class 4–6–0 No 6923 Croxteth Hall waiting to leave with a Paddington to Birkenhead train. A shunter waits alongside the three-coach set—a GWR Collett coach between two LMS brake seconds in BR maroon livery. Note the unusually long water bag and the control valve between the tracks.

braid and pork pie hat of the GWR. When the joint superintendent visited what Shrewsbury called 'The Birkenhead End' he had to show his gold medallion pass either to the ticket collectors on the interposed Great Western to Chester or on the other partner's route to Chester via Crewe.

A day out at Shrewsbury was always well spent for variety was very much the spice of railway life, change being very gradual almost to the end of steam. Platform sauntering was always civilised, with a reasonable refreshment room and plenty of chocolate machines, those tall Post Office red ones which gave a tiny bar of Nestlé's milk chocolate for a penny, or the green multi-slotted variety which produced a bar of chocolate cream, a box of Swan Vestas matches or a single Churchman's cigarette. Even the long canopied roof lasted until steam's ultimate departure in 1963.

The cause of pre-war excitement on the Crewe line was the arrival of brand new Stanier classes, blue-and-silver or red-and-gold streamlined Pacifics, single chimney Duchess Pacifics, spotless crimson Jubilees. They all arrived on stoppers waiting on the middle road until going on shed. Then there were the older classes: ex-LNWR Prince of Wales 4–6–0s from Stafford, 25648 *Queen of the Belgians*, 25725, 25775 and perhaps 25803. On the Great Western side it was mainly Knights as Kings were forbidden beyond Wolverhampton. Nationalisation brought the double chimneyed Pacifics in blue and then the newer Standards, particularly the Britannias.

89

A Great Western Mogul No 7336 (originally No 9314) stands at Welshpool station with a train for Shrewsbury via the GW/LMS joint line from Buttington Junction c1961. Following a new road-building scheme the track has been realigned on the down side of the line and the station resited, leaving the old station buildings isolated.

Added to these, both periods saw Black Fives, plus Fowler 2–6–4 tanks on the Central Wales trains via Craven Arms, Halls and Super D 0–8–0s down to Hereford and, into the 1950s, LNW 0–6–2 coal tanks or 2–4–2Ts on the Minsterley branch. The Cambrian line was also full of antiquities, Midland 0–6–0s sometimes penetrating to Welshpool, but normally GW 43XX Moguls, Manors or the antique-looking Dukedog 4–4–0s of Swindon parentage. It was quite a variety. And that leaves out one of the day's most interesting events, the tea time arrival of the West to North express worked all the way from Newton Abbot by the same Castle and enginemen—who were amazed by the size of the LMS Pacific that took over. If one were a passenger on the train before and after the Salop change, one was aware that with a different company's locomotive the whole character had changed.

13
CENTRAL FIGURE

WHO would the gaffer call to sort out a problem or ensure a special run went to time, to look after a royal visit or shepherd a party of film stars? Who would be the most enjoyable person to meet on a station platform or on a train journey, as enthusiastic as he was knowledgeable about his patch, recalling not just where every Stop Board was sited but when things had not stopped? Who would a stationmaster not quite coping with a difficult situation most welcome off the next train?

The district inspector—usually as lovable as he was venerable, able to tell a story as tall as himself (for seldom were short officials promoted to this rank), knowing everything, everybody and able instantly to pour oil on troubled waters.

You came to know where you might expect to meet him. On the first day of an accelerated famous express, he would be there to ensure departure on time and that any problem on the way was ironed out before day two. On all important occasions, there he would be, often with nothing very precise to do but reassuring by his very presence. Routinely he met all the top people, but then he routinely under-stated the importance of doing so. He shook hands but it was not for him to take glory, just to do. Seldom indeed did he appear in a photograph. If there were an accident, of course there he would be, not talking to the Press or usually even in charge of the major strategy, but quietly sorting out some subtle yet important wrinkle that would not even have occurred to a reporter.

His skill was more in knowing what not to do, when to disappear into the crowd, than in being decisive, though, make no mistake, he had the power to make or break a lesser railwayman's career. Seldom was he even vaguely in line for further promotion, for district managers did not climb up the ladder by being inspectors, and anyway usually he had only a few more years to serve. In most cases he had enjoyed a longer spell as inspector at some key junction, and unlike those new-fangled management trainees he knew all the ropes and respected what those under him were doing… and left them to get on with it as he had been allowed to at his own junction. Anyway, he never spent long enough at any one station, even the most important on his patch, to worry the local incumbent. But everyone knew he was good for a joke which might contain a sound piece of advice better heeded than ignored.

He was not, of course, a locomotive man, yet he had an extra sense that seemed to warn him when things were not quite right. No, not number such and such for the special! There was something not quite Bristol-fashion about it. He would not have to point out that his advice had been ignored if the dratted thing failed on the road!

While the gaffer might summon him at any time, he was more frequently in touch with that other unpublicised district functionary, the chief clerk, who generally held things together from inside the office and depended on him to be his eyes and ears outside. Usually they worked together, unheard of even by most of the railway's largest customers, but ensuring things happened. They did not call it good housekeeping, but that is what it was. Just occasionally chief clerk and district inspector got to loggerheads; then everything suffered. It was like the chief cook and butler not being on speaking terms.

His was an enjoyable job. Though an accident or even relatively minor incident might result in a telephone message being left at the next station he was expecting to visit—the very idea of the district inspector carrying a walkie-talkie gives him less than the dignity he deserves—generally he spent his days toing and froing to his own chosen programme. So when there was not an accelerated express, or a run of disasters, or a royal or other special, he might visit the same station five days in a row 'better to get the feel of it' or go out on the remotest branch line.

He was always looking at the detail. Detail such as whether there were any passengers still on the bridge when the porter raised his arm to tell the guard he could wave his flag? But he looked at the detail with a view to earning his keep, making passengers happy, saving unnecessary expenditure, getting the whole thing running more smoothly... distinctly not to catch someone out. Usually he was only put out by the most flagrant of abuses of safety rules, and if he were returning to the same station would make that intention known rather than arrive secretly as a spy.

Above all he loved the trains, the things they were all there to serve. He knew their history, their exact times, what locomotives came on and off where and what were the idiosyncrasies of their drivers. Seldom did he travel beyond his patch, most of the places on the destination board being unknown to him personally in the way that those who keep Heathrow running smoothly do not have to travel to all the world's other leading airports. And when he retired (and a sad day it was when he hung up his uniform) he was content to tend his garden and pay occasional visits to those on his former patch, not to get in the way of his successor but just to smile and exchange a joke... and maybe show off his onions.

14
EASTERN

THE stationmaster smoothed his lapels as he came out of his office and walked briskly down the platform, his head high in the air. Had there been an onlooker (other than a handful of railwaymen who had also stretched themselves up to their full height of importance) he would have assumed a royal train was about to pass through, or some other VIP had found his way to this rural backwater. But what was wiggling along the down track was a rake of fairly aged empty trucks, pulled by a substantial (4–6–0 tender) locomotive.

What the stationmaster was greeting was his station's first train coming to carry away the new-fangled sugar beet to the factory less than a score of miles away. For the first time in years, full use was about to be made of the station's layout and generous goods yard, where there were already great mounds of the beet and even now a further lorry load was following a horse-drawn cart piled high.

Trade has been bad. This country station, like so many, has been under-used. Fewer people went off to the sea this summer, and an improved bus service has deprived the stationmaster of his once weekly rush at the booking office, when the locals came to get the train to market. On the goods and parcels sides, too, it has long been a story of decline, and now there is something new… and on a grand scale.

After the war the streamliners did not return but the LNER continued to use their streamlined Pacific locomotives on a wide variety of 'top link' work. Class A4 No 60022 Mallard leaves platform 10 (now 8) at King's Cross with the down Tees–Tyne Pullman 4.45pm to Newcastle c1955. The coaches appear to be the 1928 stock built for the Queen of Scots service plus a post-war rebuilt bar car. The demolition of Battlebridge Road bridge which crossed the station between the signal box and the station roof until the early 1920s allowed a small locomotive servicing area including a turntable to be constructed on the right of this view.

Some neighbouring stations have been handling the sugar beet for several years now, but they don't rush into new things in this neck of the wood. Yet now, a 28-wagon train, exclusively for this station!

Looking at his watch as though to record the very moment that the last of the wagons is stowed behind the safety points, the stationmaster reflects on what else will be happening around the railway for which he works. The Flying Scotsman and two following expresses will be well clear of London, the fish from Aberdeen well on her way south, but mainly his colleagues will be moving (or organising the moving of) coal and other humdrum heavy things. Though there are three times as many passenger as freight trains passing through this station, passenger revenue is a drop in the ocean compared to the tolls on carrying freight. Every schoolboy knows that railways do not earn their profits from passengers... not, according to a recent message from headquarters, that there is much profit now anyway.

The London & North Eastern, the LNER, was perhaps the least popular of the four of the Grouping era. It has been described as a misty railway because it was hard to put it in perspective, even when we could see it... and its dirty steam engines greatly added to the mists and fogs for which much of its territory was renowned. It always seemed as busy as it was dirty, and appeared somewhat ashamed of itself. Many of its customers expected less of it than its competitors. But then much of its business was coal, over a hundred million tons of it annually, and of course that created activity and grime.

When it was formed by the merger of railways of very different character, it immediately suffered a loss of substantial volumes of traffic. As the 1920s progressed, its revenues continued to drop, and everywhere economy was the watchword. Stationmasters waited anxiously for the next visit by the dreaded 'razor gangs' cutting jobs and facilities.

The LNER never came anywhere near making a profit. Its shareholders had a miserable deal, and rebuffed the directors' plan to give themselves compensation for loss of office on nationalisation so that their pittance could be marginally increased. Well might railway historians have been incredulous when it was realised the Government was serious about privatisation in the even harsher 1990s.

When other railways built substantial numbers of new locomotives, the LNER could only afford a

Things changed slowly in East Anglia before dieselisation and Beeching, with pre-Grouping locomotives and rolling stock still comprising a large proportion of the fleet. A former GER Intermediate 2–4–0 (LNER class E4) No 62788 is caught here at Thetford station pulling a train of ex-Great Eastern coaches in April 1952. Passengers on the Norwich to Ely line could change at Thetford for branches to Swaffham and Bury St Edmunds, although in July 1953 the Bury branch was closed to passengers.

handful. It was forever making do and mending. It suffered of course because its part of Britain was hit disproportionately in the depression—the decline of heavy industry not being unique to our age.

Yet against this extraordinarily grim background the railway was actually very successful. After nationalisation, though at first the larger LMS was dominant, ultimately LNER men substantially took over all BR.

It comes as a shock to southerners to learn that by far the best of the lines that went into the LNER in 1923 was the North Eastern, built on a monopolistic control of its region's rich mining industry. The Great Northern, which met the North Eastern just north of Doncaster and ran into King's Cross, was not such a great concern, and throughout LNER days a bottleneck severely restricted traffic. The Great Eastern, serving East Anglia, was in a lower league again, best known for its intense service of steam trains for workers into Liverpool Street. The Jazz service (so called because of the colour scheme above the compartment windows denoting classes) had no equal in the world. It was effective but highly ungracious. Also taken over was the Great Central, the last main line built into London (Marylebone), with Sheffield and Manchester as its main northern traffic points. The LNER covered much of industrial Yorkshire and Lancashire, even got into North Wales, as well as being very strong in western as well as eastern Scotland. Except in the North Eastern's

Class A1 Pacific No 4481 St Simon races along the East Coast main line near Potters Bar with the down Yorkshire Pullman in the late 1930s. The mixture of streamlined and Pullman trains provided an excellent standard of service on the main LNER routes, albeit at the cost of supplementary fares. The original Gresley class A1 Pacific design was almost continuously upgraded during its lifetime, from the improved, long travel, valve gear provided in the 1920s and early 1930s to the fitting of double chimneys and smoke deflectors in the late 1950s and early 1960s.

A former GCR class J10 0–6–0 No 65131, based at Northwich (CLC) shed, rattles through the verdant surroundings of Delamere forest with a through freight of tank wagons on 10 May 1949. Note the locomotive's flower-pot chimney replacing the graceful Robinson original.

territory, it met stiff competition almost everywhere. The Marylebone service for Manchester competed against two LMS routes, and across much of the Midlands and North, LNER and LMS men glowered at each other as they picked up traffic from their rival sidings serving the same pits.

The secret of the LNER's success was largely in the appreciation of the enormity of its problem. It knew it could not effect revolutions, and sought a quiet life by avoiding the centralisation that rocked the stability of the LMS, and allowing things simply to develop. Old loyalties were encouraged by local boards mainly consisting of the former directors of the independent companies. Management meant attention to detail.

It was the quality of the detail that saved the day. Timetables were ingenious, exploiting traffic possibilities, avoiding waste. The excursion programme

was extremely successful, huge crowds being carried at such modest fares that sometimes a bus journey home from the station in the early hours of the morning would cost more than 250 miles by train. Professionalism abounded; even today you come across neat notebooks young railwaymen kept of all the management information, rules and tips—usually about the handling of humble goods traffic—they thought might further their career. The professionalism that went into operating Liverpool Street with its frequent triple simultaneous departures, each train carrying a thousand squashed-up workers, was unbelievable.

Equal enthusiasm went into the running of the long-distance freight and perishables trains, mainly running overnight and knitting substantial parts of the nation together. Even in the 1930s the Anglo-Scottish trunk services averaged over 40mph and were seldom seriously late.

Long-distance expresses began poorly. Then the LNER sprung one of its surprises. Under Nigel Gresley, one of the finest locomotive engineers the world has seen, great locomotive classes were topped by the streamlined A4s incorporating ideas from the

The original Great Northern Railway poster advertising the bracing delights of Skegness has been used so often by the railways and the local people that the jolly fisherman has become synonymous with the town. There is indeed a statue of the fisherman at the station, albeit in a rather more becalmed pose.

Skegness where it was 'so bracing', the holiday business was catered for magnificently by a rich variety of routings. The working of Scarborough station at the end of a busy bank holiday was another of the LNER's wonders of management.

That word, 'management', ever crops up in the annals of the LNER, for it was not only the first railway but the first major industrial concern to encourage formal training. Its trainees, given formal and broad practical experience, so knew their jobs that (as hinted earlier) they ultimately ended up running most of British Rail.

For the LNER they made the best of what traffic there was, and particularly exploited the agricultural revolution in East Anglia which brought much-needed business to offset industrial losses, especially in steel and shipbuilding in the North East. Milk was carried in increasing quantities, with a steady switch from churns to tankers, while trains took raw materials to the new canning and bottling plants and brought away the finished products. Sugar beet

racing car Bugattis. The LNER workshops employed 50,000 men, mainly engaged in very routine work, but there was room for a touch of quality and each of the streamliners was lovingly, individually handbuilt.

By the outbreak of war, many long-distance expresses had been revolutionised, and the Silver Jubilee set passenger standards never excelled in Britain. Backed by sharp publicity, including famous posters talking of the drier side of Britain and

Overleaf above **East Coast Elegance**
One of the most noteworthy and best-documented events in Britain's railway history was Mallard's *world record breaking exploit when 126mph was reached at milepost 90¼ on the East Coast main line on 3 July 1938. To commemorate the 50th anniversary of this marvellous achievement, the artist wished to produce a somewhat different painting. It needed to convey the elegance, power and speed of Sir Nigel Gresley's A4 Pacifics. Not wishing to show the engine actually breaking the record, as this had been done before, he decided on a low viewpoint, such as one might enjoy from the lineside, featuring those attractive red driving wheels. Drawings were made at the National Railway museum at York with the Grantham elements added later in the studio. The approaching A4 restarting a northbound express shows the characteristic front end of these magnificent machines.*

Overleaf below **Gateshead Winter**
Eastern region class A3 No 60071 Tranquil—*what a lovely name—heaves its southbound East Coast express across the River Tyne off the King Edward bridge passing Gateshead engine shed during the early sixties. Designed by Nigel Gresley, and built at the North British locomotive works in 1924 as London & North Eastern No 2570, she is depicted here in final condition with a double chimney and German-style smoke deflectors which gave this otherwise typical British design a decidedly alien air. She was withdrawn from service by BR in October 1964. One of the most famous British locomotives,* Flying Scotsman, *is now the sole survivor of this class and during 1993 was returned to traffic in the form seen here as opposed to the apple green livery previously carried.*

Philip D. Hawkins

The Cornishman

During the late fifties, and until 1962, the artist would often be perched on his bicycle on Tyseley bridge at 6.30 on summer evenings to watch the Cornishman curve off the North Warwickshire line to join the main line and continue its journey through to Birmingham Snow Hill. Having left Penzance at 10.30am, the train was taken over by a Wolverhampton Stafford Road Castle engine at Bristol. By the time it came into view at Tyseley, it would invariably be running late. The painting, however, shows the southbound train drifting through Knowle & Dorridge station. Though the usual route was via the North Warwickshire line, leaving the main line at Tyseley, occasionally this route leaving the main line at Hatton North junction was taken. Everything was changed in 1962 when The Cornishman was rerouted via the ex-Midland Railway through Cheltenham and Birmingham New Street. Memories of the real Cornishman are vivid. The locomotive seen here is Stafford Road Castle No 7026 Tenby Castle. *Note the smart set of Mark 1 coaches in chocolate-and-cream.*

proved a lifesaver; all but two of the nineteen factories run by the British Sugar Corporation were on LNER territory. It is interesting to note, however, that even in LNER days there were comments about increasing imports of manufactured goods—even German beer—through Harwich and other ports. The LNER docks were the largest in single ownership, though the Great Western's handled much more cargo.

Holding the LNER together in peace was a sizeable challenge. The war brought triumphant handling of new traffic (even more sugar beet until Britain became sugar self-sufficient): materials for building numerous aerodromes in East Anglia and the fuel and bombs for the planes, and everywhere far more passengers. Then the very world seemed to fall apart: the coal-led world, anyway. Labour shortages led to coal shortages and a shocking reduction in quality and reliability. Drivers and firemen had an ever more miserable time keeping the ageing wheels moving. In the railway's last harsh winter of 1947, coal ran out at depots like Neasden, and morale collapsed with crews simply not turning up for duty.

The state indeed inherited a poor set of assets, much worse from the LNER than the other three. In truth the company would have gone bankrupt within a couple of years had the government not intervened in some way... yet, after Labour had been swept to power in 1945, it was the LNER that led the antinationalisation campaign, suggesting the government provide the tracks and private enterprise run the trains—again a fashionable idea.

The challenge facing the Eastern Region in 1948 was immense. For a start, the LNER was distributed between three Regions. Lines north of the border naturally went to the Scottish Region, while as we shall see later the North East was given back its independence to face its own problems and make the most of its considerable potential. The Great Central lines which had continued to be run with considerable independence in LNER days were chopped and changed but ultimately all lost. That left the Eastern essentially running things out of King's Cross and Liverpool Street (and later Fenchurch Street), and they went no better together than things spun off elsewhere. Indeed well after the North Eastern Region had been merged into the Eastern, and only shortly before Regions were abolished in favour of sectorisation, a separate East Anglian Region was formed to help give the railways of the region a better local identity.

After nationalisation, not surprisingly, the general manager based at Liverpool Street had two chief lieutenants: the line manager (Great Northern) at King's Cross and the line manager (Great Eastern) also based at Liverpool Street. There never really was an Eastern Region style like there had been an LNER one. And while the LNER's board (chaired by the present Lord Whitelaw's grandfather) resembled a *Who's Who* of British industry, the Regional personnel were little known outside the industry.

They were, however, as tough as they were well trained, and never underestimated their task. They ran quite a few of the trains we most loved as well as being more ruthless in pruning than the management of any other Region. In the LNER tradition, resources continued to be used imaginatively. Pruning, however, meant not just leaving substantial tracts of East Anglia without rails and thinning out wayside stations but running sparser local services than was the norm elsewhere.

The upheaval in the early days of nationalisation was enormous. Two big pluses were the completion of the Liverpool Street suburban electrification and the elimination of the Potter's Bar bottleneck on the East Coast main line. A minus was the rapid loss of much of the agricultural traffic the LNER had successfully built up in East Anglia, while the determined effort to retain long-distance freight to the North merely delayed its decline. What had been essentially a freight railway was turned by the biggest transition of all into a mainly passenger one.

The trains we especially remember are the East Coast main line ones hauled by Gresley's Pacifics, able to sustain front-line duty for an amazing period. Of course readers will look for a picture of a streamlined A4. What machines they were and what splendid journeys they gave! The number of fast expresses to the North also increased. And when dieselisation came, earlier than on most main lines, there were the Deltics resplendent in their special two-tone green livery (they did not go blue until the 1970s). As that great railway photographer Bishop Treacy said, if you had to have diesels then at least the Deltics had character and were worth recording. In a later age, more people turned out for the last Deltic run than have ever done so for a steam event. Now Peterborough was regularly being passed from London in less than an hour.

Meanwhile things had been transformed out of all recognition on the run from Liverpool Street to Norwich. Elsewhere British Rail standard classes at best met with a mixed reception, and on the Western the powerful Britannias were so disliked as often to be abused. Eastern men loved them. Never before had such power been available on the difficult East Anglian run, or such pride been displayed in attaining speed and reliability.

Many had affection, too, for the Cambridge buffet car expresses (out of King's Cross) while nowhere in Britain was a better dinner served on a train than in platform 9 at Liverpool Street on the boat express for the Hook of Holland night service; the journey being short, it was necessary to start serving before departure. We also fondly look back to the days of through trains from King's Cross to numerous East Coast resorts, the Broadsman with its restaurant car for Cromer (Beach) being an especial favourite. Comparing services to the resorts of today with those of the first decade of the Eastern Region makes one truly nostalgic. Liverpool Street was ever fascinating

A Robinson class A5 4–6–2T No 69820 heads an interesting collection of carriages forming the 1.45pm New Holland Pier to Immingham service on 3 June 1952. Trains to Immingham and Cleethorpes connected with the Humber ferries from Hull Corporation Pier. The paddle steamer Lincoln Castle—*seen in the background—departed Hull at 1.15pm arriving at New Holland 20 minutes later. The Pier branch and ferry service closed from 25 June 1981, with the opening of the Humber Bridge.*

Overleaf **Sunshine & Steam**
Chocolate-and-cream coaches hauled by copper and brass clad locomotives carrying attractive headboards will always be synonymous to the artist with summer holidays in the fifties. A fortnight's holiday at Dawlish would be spent almost entirely watching the trains go by. The Torbay Express, the Mayflower, the Royal Duchy, The Cornishman and the Cornish Riviera Express must remain etched into many memories. Here No 6023 King Edward II *begins its stately progress along the promenade at Dawlish beneath the distinctive red sandstone cliffs. Semaphore signalling remained along this route until as late as 1987. No 6023 is presently undergoing restoration at Didcot with plans to return it to single chimney condition.*

and never more so than on a Saturday morning when from the café on the bridge you could see expresses to a host of seaside destinations leaving from platforms normally the preserve of suburban services.

So much closed so quickly, including the greatest casualty of all, the Midland & Great Northern from Peterborough to Yarmouth (under pressure on summer Saturdays till the very end), that those of us living in other parts of the country could not possibly catch it all. A few of the surviving oddities in a region once noted for them we did catch—especially New Holland Pier where we saw trucks of coal shunted to the pier head to provide fuel for the railway-owned paddle steamer across the Humber and watched trains departing for Barton-on-Humber (the ultimate get-away-from-it destination), Cleethorpes and

The 22 Deltic diesels replaced the streamlined A4s on the top east coast duties from 1961 and allowed significant accelerations to take place. No 9008 The Green Howards stands under the magnificent roof of York station with a King's Cross–Edinburgh service in the early 1970s. To the left a Peak class 45 1Co-Co1 No 24 has brought in what looks to be a schools' special. The introduction of the full High Speed Train service on the East Coast route in the late 1970s brought the end of the Deltic era, with the final withdrawals taking place early in 1982. York became the headquarters of an enlarged Eastern Region, combining the former Eastern and North Eastern Regions, at the beginning of 1967.

Immingham Docks. By changing from the Cleethorpes train at Grimsby (Town) you could get to that railway crossroads, Spalding, via Louth and Boston. And so on almost ad infinitum.

15
PADDINGTON–
ST IVES

THE train speeds across the timeless Exminster marshes and brakes hard as it enters the first of many curves, with the Exe estuary on one side, the village of Lympstone with its clock tower opposite, and Powderham Castle and its deer on the other. It winds along the estuary through Starcross with Brunel's atmospheric tower (one of the few remnants of the not wholly unsuccessful attempt to drive trains by vacuum power) and then out alongside the open sea at Dawlish Warren.

Hundreds of thousands of adults and children have caught their first glimpse of the waves here, and one still remembers the ecstasy in the crowded compartments of trains on peak summer Saturdays in the late 1940s, taking families on their first holidays with pay. This surely, we thought, was the dawn of a new age.

Then along the ledge daringly built under the red sandstone cliffs and over a short viaduct where Dawlish Water tumbles into the sea; Dawlish's station, perched on the sea's edge, is periodically damaged in storms. In and out of four short tunnels and one slightly longer one, and along the main Sea Wall (it deserves its capitals) for a couple of enchanted miles where even the reserved English cross to the other side to gain a better view. Since the 1840s this has been the romantic and fastest practical route for many west-bound travellers on journeys of every conceivable kind, all taking in the panorama of cliffs, rocks, waves. Even the cliffs have changed their shape gradually over that time and, except that it is still the permanent way, the railway has been revolutionised several times over. The first trains were not only broad gauge but atmospheric hauled. Instead of an engine they had a piston carriage, the piston fitting within a large pipe laid between the rails: vacuum in front, air let in behind to provide the driving force.

Then a glimpse of Teignmouth sea front and pier as the route switches inland, past busy Teignmouth harbour where trucks used to be pushed round the sidings by a curious road steamer called *The Elephant*, and up the Teign estuary—like a lake at high tide, a bird sanctuary at low, with villages nestling under the red and green hills opposite and a clear glimpse of Hay Tor as Newton Abbot racecourse is passed.

Hardened businessmen, American tourists, even those whose daily trek to work in this way, all love these miles and cherish favourite memories of storms (rough seas do sometimes stop the wheels and trains have occasionally had to take shelter in a tunnel), sunrises and perfect summer's days when thousands of small craft decorate the scene. But in truth the Sea Wall is only one highlight on a journey of outstanding interest all the way from Paddington to furthest Cornwall, over three hundred miles. The steam-hauled, Cornish Riviera Express might have taken nearly 1½ hours longer

Overleaf **Heading West**
Clun Castle *is well known today as a preserved engine but in the fifties it was just another Castle allocated to Newton Abbot shed and was often used on cross-country expresses. The location here is Starcross where, for many 'townies', the artist included, summer holidays really began. This was where the sea could first be seen across the Exe estuary. The train would soon be passing through Dawlish Warren, Dawlish and Teignmouth to allow holidaymakers a sneak preview of their well-deserved break. Many Midlanders had their first sight of the sea with noses pressed against windows of The Cornishman's chocolate-and-cream carriages. During a short break in the summer of 1991 the artist took the opportunity to visit the location to collect necessary reference for this painting. Little had changed over the years except for details such as guest-house signs sprouting from the houses on the left. The Castles single chimney is a reminder that Clun's countenance was somewhat different from its preservation form.*

105

than today's service but the journey of adventure to the furthest west was surely never a moment too long.

Our King class locomotive takes its time to get up speed on leaving Paddington, but is doing 85mph through Sonning Cutting along Brunel's original speedway to Bristol when the brakes go on for the junction just beyond Reading. Here we enter a rural world through which the route comprises a series of upgraded branch lines joined together by short cuts built late in railway history. The railway is totally absorbed into the changing landscape, and in over a hundred miles the largest town through which we pass is Newbury, and only one factory (the cement one at Westbury—and then most people will be looking for the white horses on the other side) intrudes on the scene in over an hour.

For the rest it is the ever-peaceful Kennet & Avon Canal—a pity the railway killed that—thatched villages, brooks, occasional lush valleys, twists and turns down a steeper valley through Bruton, woods and pheasants, even foxes seeing the train as no more threat than the plane overhead... the very essence of the English countryside. There are changes, yes, but even in the 1990s the route gives the lie to the statement that all southern England is overcrowded.

After using the Castle Cary cut-off, built in 1906 to complete today's

Old Oak Common shed was some three miles out of Paddington so a servicing point at Ranelagh Bridge provided facilities for locomotives requiring a quick turnaround at the station. A glance to see which locomotives were receiving attention here was the enthusiast's first priority on leaving Paddington. King class 4–6–0 No 6011 King James I *passes Ranelagh Bridge with a northbound express around 1950, when it was carrying early BR blue livery.*

shorter route, we join a section of the former Bristol & Exeter Railway's Yeovil branch to cross the wetlands where the economy depends on willow growing... and note the Isle of Athelney. We pass under the down Bristol line at Cogload Junction and race down the quadrupled track through Taunton and on to Norton Fitzwarren. It is here, where the two down tracks become one for the climb up Wellington Bank, that many holidaymakers experience their trains queuing signal to signal on summer Saturdays: 'We raced to Taunton and then it was stop, stop, stop'.

Our weekday Cornish Riviera is however given a clear run, though soon our speed which has so far averaged over a mile a minute all the way from Paddington drops to 30mph as we enter Whiteball Tunnel, separating Somerset from Devon. We touch 90mph on the descent through Tiverton Junction and Cullompton, braking for the curve just beyond the latter. The home but not the distant signals are off at Cowley Bridge Junction, where up Southern trains join down Western ones, but almost at once Exeter St David's is ready for us, road traffic halted at the level crossing by Middle Box, and we accelerate through the middle down road noticing a Western train waiting to follow us on one side and a Southern waiting to climb to Central on the other.

Then the magic of salt water between Exeter and Newton Abbot already described. The big question is whether to stop at Newton for a pilot engine; given our ten-coach formation, that is at the discretion of our driver who will have given the appropriate advance indication probably by whistle to St David's West Box. Good: we are going through, noticing that the up Cornish Riviera is also running through non-stop, overtaking the Kingswear section of the Cornishman for Wolverhampton. That gives us a good start up Dainton Bank, though we are down to 20mph before the tunnel, avoiding slipping in it. Down to sea level at Totnes and another stiff climb up through Tigley until we meet with the Dartmoor foothills and enjoy a fine view over the rich farmlands toward the South Hams. All the way we have had a copy of the GWR's *Through the Window* open and note each junction, wondering if we will ever get to travel to places like Shepton Mallet, Hemyock and Kingsbridge. You can feel the plunge down Hemerdon Bank to Plympton. There are still ten minutes to reach Plymouth North Road. We pass along the Plym estuary, white with the workings of the china clay trade, and see an interesting range of locomotives at Laira.

But we leave Mutley Tunnel at walking speed and come to a stand before being allowed into the platform, barely on time. Many trains that arrive punctually outside Bristol, Exeter and Plymouth are let in late. The Western has the reputation for good work out on the road but lousy station discipline. The King cuts off and we lose three coaches, the remaining seven including restaurant car to which we will move once our Castle is on and we are away. On the platform we feel exhilarated that we have reached Plymouth in four hours non-stop, but there are still nearly 80 miles to go. Only five minutes are allowed for the engine change and, surprise, that is exceeded and we are 1½ minutes late leaving, delaying the departure of a Southern stopper to Exeter. A stopper from Exeter arrives as we leave. It passed through St David's 1 hour 20 minutes before we did and is again travelling in the opposite direction to us. Both these Southern trains have Moguls at the head of

Overleaf above **Grey Day at Paddington**
This view from the country end of platform 1 at Paddington was mainly only known to railwaymen and those members of the public with rather more than a passing interest in railways. Today this view is virtually the same but time has seen a drastic change in motive power with HST 125s taking the place of such stately locomotives as this Castle No 7027 Thornbury Castle *at the head of an express for Worcester. It was built at Swindon in BR days in 1949 and withdrawn from service in 1963. After languishing with many other withdrawn engines at Barry in South Wales for several years, it was rescued and removed to Tyseley in the late sixties. But for a brief sojourn on the Dart Valley Railway, it has remained there for over 25 years but is now the subject of a restoration appeal.*

Above **Racing the Storm**

The most vivid recollections of freight trains are not so much visual as audible, particularly the sounds of buffers clanging and brake levers shuddering. This elderly Churchward 2–8–0 No 2819 is hurrying a class F express freight along the down main-shaking the station furniture at Acocks Green & South Yardley in the southern suburbs of Birmingham. The period is the late fifties and, when withdrawn from service in January 1961, No 2819 was over fifty years old. By any standards it had given excellent value for money. The footbridge in the background was well trodden by the artist in the sixties when many railway adventures began and ended here. Home was just a mile or so away.

Opposite below **Early Shift**

A scene in the late fifties at St Ives in Cornwall. Small Prairie No 4566 is prepared for the day's work ahead outside the tiny, ancient engine shed. This particular locomotive survived the scrapyard into preservation along with several of its type. The St Ives branch left the main line at St Erth and came into its own during the summer months, particularly in the fifties, with an ever-increasing influx of holidaymakers. The line survives today, one of the few branch lines in Cornwall to do so, with 'park and ride' schemes helping to alleviate the chronic car parking problem at St Ives.

Exeter St Davids, meeting place of the Great Western and Southern routes to the far west, always provided an interesting spectacle. A Newton Abbot (83A) based Castle 4–6–0 No 5024 Carew Castle *heads a Saturday holiday train from Manchester to Paignton (reporting No 212) on 6 August 1955. The stock is provided by the London Midland Region and Western Region motive power will have taken over at Bristol.*

Opposite below *The fearsome South Devon banks, a legacy of the atmospheric system, presented the steam locomotive with a formidable test. Here Laira-based King class 4–6–0 No 6025* King Henry III, *having tackled the shorter eastbound climb, including a stretch at 1 in 37, coasts down Dainton Bank at Stoneycombe c1949 with an up express. No 6025 is in the short-lived BR experimental blue colour lined out in red, cream and grey.*

rakes of LSWR non-corridor coaches with occasional lavatories between compartments.

The Cornish Riviera is now surprisingly lightly loaded. While some joined at Plymouth, more are waiting for the Saltash auto-car and the following Cornishman which makes more stops. They call this the Cornish Riviera, but in truth it serves only a small part of the Royal Duchy. Only a dozen are taking afternoon tea.

Our teacake is already being served as we cross Brunels' masterpiece, the Royal Albert Bridge over the Tamar. Then that wonderful game of hide and seek with salt water, the view from the viaduct at St German's being specially rewarding. Non-stop through Liskeard (afternoon sandwiches), Bodmin Road (brown bread and butter) and Lostwithiel (fruit cake and a hot water top up), our first halt (and only the second since Paddington!) is at Par, where a handful of people get out for the connecting train. In less than an hour there will be another connection for the Cornishman. Along the cliffs and we race through St Austell, which is one of the line's busiest traffic points but not prestigious enough for us, and slow for Truro having taken in the detail of the cathedral.

A lot is happening at Truro, but apart from the fact they are anxious to despatch us it all seems a bit leisurely. We are due in at 4.03pm and due out three minutes later. But the local from here to Penzance with a Hall standing at the far side of the opposite island does not come to life till 4.15 and the Falmouth train in the bay beside us (a standard GWR two-coach branch-line set with a Prairie tank) follows three minutes after that. The traffic people are surely manipulating the statistics: they claim how quick we are

The Sea Wall between Dawlish and Teignmouth is still a highlight of any rail journey to the South West today. It has been a favourite spot of railway photographers through the years. In this late morning view taken from the promenade Castle class 4–6–0 No 5090 Neath Abbey approaches Teignmouth with the 5.30am Paddington to Plymouth and Penzance, via Bristol, 'Newspaper train' on 23 February 1951. This service was due into Penzance at 4.25pm, a marathon journey taking as long as the overnight sleepers. Its nickname dates from the days London newspapers left London in the early hours rather than late in the evening previous to publication date.

and how few trains are late; but even if we were ten minutes down the connections would comfortably reach their destinations on time. And as for those going to Perranporth, they have to cross over the bridge at Truro to get the local and change again at Chacewater with another 13 minutes wait there. It undoubtedly makes you feel special going to the far west. Yet we feel almost guilty dashing through Redruth and Camborne which served the industrial revolution so well and now form a single urban district with far more people than anywhere this train now serves. We sail through to Gwinear Road.

That might not be so ridiculous had not the three people changing there had to wait nearly half an hour for the branch train to Helston to get started... after the arrival of the stopper from Truro! We now see the white sands of Hayle and descend to St Erth where we change. An up train has just left, but it would seem to be too obvious to run a smart connection out of both it and the Cornish Riviera. We have to wait 13 minutes. Our mixed rake of corridor and non-corridor coaches hauled by another Prairie tank then shows off its superior role connecting with the day's best train from Paddington by being the only weekday service to miss Lelant Halt. Frustration about poor connections—the inevitable belief that we could organise it better—was always part of the enjoyment! But rounding the cliffs through Carbis Bay and on to St Ives any lingering negative feeling evaporates as the clouds, blue sea and white sands take our all.

Our only possible regret is that we have travelled on a weekday. On Saturdays the Cornish Riviera itself comes here. St Erth is then only second top (Truro the first) from Paddington, yet without change St Ives is reached half an hour later. No. We were right to miss the congestion but will photograph Saturday's arrival at what the stationmaster lovingly still calls Great Western on Sea.

The views across the bay open out to give a marvellous climax as journey's end at St Ives is reached. The 2.15pm from St Erth arrives at the terminus, 15 minutes later, behind GWR prairie tank No 4549 on Friday 4 August 1961. Another 4500 class 2–6–2 tank No 4570 stands in the bay platform. The small engine shed which closed at the end of the 1961 summer timetable can be seen beyond the last coach.

16
SUMMER

FOR thousands of railwaymen, railway enthusiasts, and those who simply used trains or depended on them for their business, the arrival of the summer timetable was a moment of excitement, even passion. Many staff could instantly tell what extra hours they might be working, and so what extra pay they would take home. Stationmasters jealously compared the services at their station with neighbouring and comparable ones. Everyone in the holiday business, but especially those responsible for publicity and attracting the visitors, could see what the railway was doing for their resort as opposed to rivals. Enthusiasts looked for accelerations, more Saturday trains (with restaurant cars working down more single-line branches) and oddities such as unbalanced workings or the repetition of a previous timing mistake. Regular travellers looked forward to faster, more comfortable journeys.

The traffic people had of course been conducting consultations since the levels of last summer's loadings had been noted, and timetable proofs had been circulated from top brass to stationmasters. But proofs were proofs and there could be all manner of changes. Even rumours of a new through Friday night train, or of a service experimentally introduced last summer not being repeated, could be awry. And while the public relations department put out their usual plugs, inevitably these selectively highlighted the gloss rather than the substance.

There was no moment in the railway calendar quite like the arrival of the finished timetable and having the joy or frustration of reviewing the detail that affected you. Most major service improvements, such as the further acceleration of key trains, began with the summer timetable which made it more glamorous than the winter one, quite apart from the fact that many more trains ran in summer. A growing number of branch as well as main lines were given separate summer Saturday tables, and scores of lines only saw Sunday trains in season.

Before the war timetables appeared as punctually as the crack trains they highlighted in their preliminary pages. During the war even the smallest stations received their copies on the dot, though the quantity printed was drastically reduced and you had to reserve yours well in advance. Though all railways but the Great Western now used reprints of the relevant pages from *Bradshaw*, each retained its individual preliminary pages with such items as summary tables (generously showing what the opposition also provided as between London and Birmingham or Wolverhampton). Until its last pre-nationalisation issue, 6 October 1947 (and until further notice) the Great Western retained its traditional 11½in by 7½in format and its own consistent but idiosyncratic system of notes (G for Saturdays excepted) for sixpence.

The 'until further notice' belonged to the age of austerity... austerity that was to be intensified during that winter's timetable and which would delay the steady progression to normality in the first summer of state ownership. Alas, having timetables appear punctually did not become the norm for years to come, their lateness (and their subjection to massive changes announced in supplements) being cited as one example of how nationalisation had resulted in the public being treated with less respect. One of the 1950s bouts of economies was indeed inflicted at short notice a couple of weeks after the summer timetable had begun, resulting in massive inconvenience since, even if you checked out every train against the supplement and so knew what was running, the service on many routes was erratic.

Yet there were few lines in holiday areas that did not both have their best train service and carry their largest numbers of passengers well into BR days. The postwar explosion of holidays with pay led first to an enormous strain on resources, then to an increase in those resources and finally (as road competition began to bite) a determined effort to stay in business. So the arrival of the summer timetable retained its focal interest. Now there were six Regions, to get the whole picture you needed to invest a small fortune, especially since in most parts of Britain that meant sending for some by post. The mechanics were awful, but the messages inside stimulating.

Starlight Specials, car-carrying trains, a sleeper to Penzance exclusively for the use of Scilly Isles passengers, an increasing range of overnight services from the Midlands, North and Scotland to the South West... the catalogue is extensive even before turning to daytime trains. You could spend an enjoyable hour tracing the routes (including curves only used by the summer Saturday holiday trains) taken by services to and from Filey Holiday camp, whose station was at the apex of a triangle just off the Scarborough–Hull line. Many trains reached it without touching either Scarborough or Hull. The London Midland Region timetable's preliminary pages included a whole succession of cross-country services: London, Manchester and Sheffield to Ipswich and Harwich; Manchester, Stoke-on-Trent and Birmingham, and also East Midland cities to Brighton, Eastbourne, Bexhill and Hastings; Birkenhead to Margate and Sandwich; Manchester and Liverpool and Bradford and Leeds to Bournemouth both via the Somerset & Dorset; Birkenhead and Birmingham Snow Hill to Bournemouth via Oxford and Basingstoke. In its last days the Midland & Great Northern was as busy as the Somerset & Dorset, while some lines that had nominally closed (Tebay to Kirkby Stephen for example) carried Saturday expresses. But then the whole of the Midlands and industrial North were criss-crossed by routes, many normally freight only, that carried trains on their way to the sea. Castleford in Yorkshire was among the scores of uninspiring places at which such summer Saturday services tended to linger to take water or for crew or signalling purposes.

As carrying the increasing crowds of holidaymakers became more sophisticated, supposedly non-stop runs became more exotic: Paddington to Truro, Newton Abbot to Burton-on-Trent. Village stations were now being closed during the core of the Saturday rush, while some branch line trains (such as the Teign Valley's) were terminated short of the main line and passengers bussed into civilisation to prevent interrupting the flow of

Leaflets issued in the West Midlands retained a pre-nationalisation style into the 1950s. Ex-GWR or LMS services were easily identified.

expresses. All this and much more we could deduce from the summer timetable, perhaps devouring our own Region's volume hot off the press with a bar of chocolate lying on the bed, ignoring more mundane tasks.

Many people turned out to see some new or accelerated train on the first day of the timetable, usually in mid-June, though it varied according to the nation's economy and BR's mood. We of course knew that all the famous things, like the GWR running the world's longest non-stop train from Paddington to Plymouth, happened on previous first days of the summer timetable. Before and after the war, the day meant the reopening of seasonal signalboxes, shortening the sections on some branch lines (those controlling two passing loops on the Minehead branch) as well as main ones such as between Exeter and Newton Abbot. It also meant station staff posting up the new timetable in its poster form and neatly underlining entries for their own trains.

More important, extra locomotives were allocated for summer passenger

Summer weekends, and Saturdays in particular, saw all sorts of motive power pressed into passenger service. A class 8F 2–8–0 No 48629 of Willesden shed (1A) awaits departure at the south end of York station on Saturday 5 September 1959 with a train of LMS stock, possibly from Scarborough. The locomotive will have been particularly interesting to the spotters on the left as it was a wartime example built by the Southern Railway at Brighton, in 1943. In addition, it has a smaller Midland pattern tender.

duties, while new carriages were hastily put into service and rakes of old ones that had hardly turned a wheel since last summer again readied. Before and after the war, the range of destination boards (some used less than a dozen occasions a year) grew steadily. Many railwaymen who reached retirement age earlier in the year were asked to stay on till September, while school leavers entering the railway profession were expected to start immediately. Just everything and everybody was needed for the coming rush.

The performance on the timetable's first day, always a Monday, was given special review… and on the six and nine o'clock news bulletins we expected to hear about the latest accelerations. VIPs were often carried on first runs. Space was usually plentiful, for the arrival of the augmented summer timetable did not automatically bring a huge increase in business compared with the previous weeks. The best journeys of all were in the early days of the summer timetable when everything was sparkling new but not taxed by peak season crowds. Without the need to run extras and split service trains into two or three, even the first Saturdays often went off smoothly. Do you recall in your entire life a holiday season whose business did not start unusually slowly?

At least until the end of the 1950s, the one thing never lacking in high summer was customers. What days they were, especially the summer Saturdays when record crowds were carried by day and night by a huge variety of routes and power was provided by a rich range of pre-Grouping, Grouping and BR Standard locomotives, freight as well as passenger. Though our elders might boast that in their childhood holiday trains were still more varied, especially in the liveries of their carriages, we had the advantage of far heavier traffic: more trains and heavier trains made possible

Blackpool expanded rapidly in the last century, with the visitors brought by the railways, to become the busiest holiday town in the country. Two large stations, Blackpool North and Blackpool Central, were required to handle the traffic from all over the country, but particularly workers from the Lancashire mill towns. This early 1930s view taken at Central is dominated by the famous tower opened in 1894 and shows a L&Y rebuilt Aspinall class 3F 0–6–0 No 12560, based at Blackpool Central shed (C32), shunting empty stock.

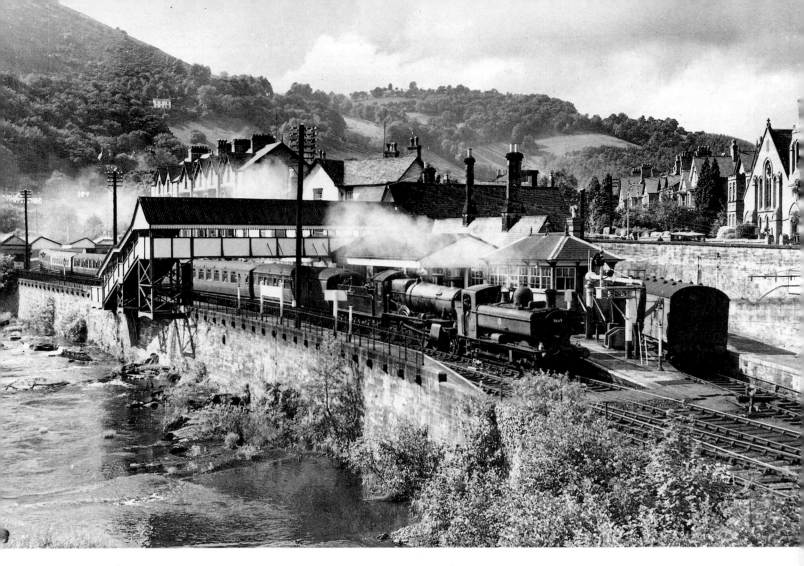

by the steady increase in power of the average locomotive. Of course there was never such a thing as the 'average', but these were indeed the days that drivers and firemen were frequently delighted to have a more powerful machine than in previous seasons. While today's speed is rationed mainly in terms of track and signalling capacity, with only occasional speed restrictions, most of the trains we loved went as fast as the steam locomotives could take them with reasonable economy in coal consumption. The cry was always for bigger engines. With 300 new steam locomotives coming out of BR's works annually (by 1954 three-quarters of them in BR's own classes) the power/weight ratio steadily improved. Yet double heading remained prevalent on many routes in summer, almost universal on some summer Saturdays… and our memory of the Lickey incline is perhaps of a 2P 4–4–0 piloting a Black Five and being banked by two LMS 0–6–0 tanks at snail's pace.

Mountains of Passengers' Luggage in Advance, the everlasting business of reserving seats or obtaining Regulation tickets where they were necessary, the standard Saturday restaurant car lunch of salad already laid on the table followed by cold dessert and coffee (whole trains of restaurant cars worked down to holiday areas on Fridays, each car to feed three or four sittings on a separate Saturday train back), most unusual pairings of locomotives, destination boards turned round to expose their blank side since not all stations

Holidaymakers returning from Butlins camp at Pwllheli enjoy the scenery of the Dee valley at Llangollen in the early 1950s. A class 5700 0–6–0 Pannier tank No 9669 pilots an unknown Manor class 4–6–0 on a train of ex-LNER carriages heading back across the country. Preservation, by the Llangollen Railway, has ensured this evocative GWR view is still intact today.

advertised were served on Saturdays, train reporting numbers displayed on the front of locomotives, and some trains—usually the same ones!—running seriously late and delaying the start of returning ones: for anyone remotely interested in railways, summer Saturdays were a joy. Many, like Ivo Peters out filming the Somerset & Dorset as though it were a major sporting event (as indeed it was) each Saturday, lived them to the full. But there was so much pure entertainment provided throughout Britain that unless you specialised in one route you could only scratch the surface.

Less happy were many of the travellers for whom the whole show was provided. Even the best trains running to time took longer on the road than on Mondays to Fridays, and at the weekends straddling the old Bank Holiday first Monday in August the average journey was abysmal... and expensive. In hindsight the railways should not have carried everyone wishing to travel on peak days but rationed what could sensibly be provided, so forcing the staggering of holidays. Sadly, it was only when people travelled by car and got caught in huge traffic jams that staggering happened. Then the accountants discovered that over a seventh of BR's total revenue went to maintain its enormous passenger fleet (in some years more new passenger coaches were built than today's total InterCity stock). Though even today summer Saturdays have their interest, the great days ended early in the 1960s. Most routes saw their peak holiday loads in 1958 or 1959.

But summers were not only about Saturdays. That bargain of bargains, the Runabout ticket enabled us to explore our own area or the district in which we were holidaying. Remember how we pored over the timetable to get the most mileage, the longest time on the sands? And on every day except Saturdays there was an incredible range of long-distance excursions, a hundred miles each way for a half day on some distant sands not being the least unusual. North Wales had its circular Land Cruise, Ireland its Radio Train, and for those not actually staying by the sea, many big cities had a peak season train named after them allowing day trips to a different resort every day with the same guaranteed seat throughout. Especially on Sundays, tens of thousands arrived at resorts with the sandiest beaches from the nearest city and towns, literally over 10,000 identical tickets (as between Preston and Blackpool, York and Scarborough, Exeter St Thomas and Dawlish Warren) within a few hours.

It was always sad when Pwllheli saw its last through trains to London (separately for Paddington and Euston) depart and the Lakes Express ceased running for another season. For many of us the railways spelt summer and holidays and we remain everlastingly glad our parents were not early into the car thing and even allowed us to risk smuts in our eyes by putting our head out of the window to see the locomotive at work, and certainly granted us the freedom of the corridor from which to see our own country pass by.

Summer was of course also about people going to and from our country and others, the Channel ports being at their peak and the *Queens* needing three trains from Waterloo to Southampton for their weekly service to New York. And about fresh produce including everlasting tomatoes from the Channel Islands, plums from Pershore, a rich range of fresh things from the Garden of England, early potatoes from Pembrokeshire.

And if there is a single summer image stronger than others it must be of the newly-mown embankment catching fire as a hardworking steam locomotive showers it with sparks. We watch the gang of half a dozen wield their scythes and hooks thinking that theirs is not a bad life spent (at least when it is sunny) in pleasant conditions and minimal supervision. These are the chaps who weeks earlier were painting stations. The sound of an A1 on a heavy cross-country service gives them excuse to mop their brows and pause... though it must be three minutes before the engine passes them. They watch the receding tail lamp as though they had never seen one before, and only when it is again silent does the smell of burning dry grass make them turn. Well, they would probably have set light to it later on, so why not take advantage of the situation. Soon a hundred yards of the embankment is burning and smoke almost envelopes the following train, a mineral job hauled in plodding style by a NER 0–6–0. The gang gathers outlying vegetation and ensures all is consumed before moving on. All is ready for next spring's flowers.

A BR-built Castle class 4–6–0 No 7025 Sudeley Castle is about to depart its home town of Shrewsbury with the up Cambrian Coast Express in summer 1962. The BR dark green livery (with lining only slightly modified from the final GWR version) in combination with the chocolate-and-cream coach gives a nostalgic reflection of the old Great Western, which was already being swept away by management changes at this date. Only a few years later this classic GWR holiday train was to become a London Midland Region train worked by electric motive power out of Euston.

17

TRENT VALLEY IN THE FIFTIES

The Trent valley in 1938. Two miles north of Bellamoor LNWR signals dominate the south end of the station at Colwich, the junction for the North Stafford line to Stoke-on-Trent. An LNWR 'Cauliflower' 0–6–0 goods locomotive leaves with a three-coach local train, probably for Rugby.

THERE was certainly an element of luck in having a base in Rugeley, a few miles south-east of Stafford and within earshot of the Trent Valley line. Bellamoor Bridge was the principal haunt, close to milepost 125 out of Euston and about a mile north of Rugeley Trent Valley station. We went along a footpath beside the waterworks and then down the steps to the towpath by the cut, to the Trent & Mersey Canal, whose aqueduct over the River Trent was in sight of the railway but still a quarter of a mile away. A train would rush past in the distance with an apparently interesting loco at its head, but its number? Anybody's guess. If it was a slow goods, though, a run for it might bring dividends. It was all part of the fun. On one such dash, luck was on the side of the good and breathless. The loco turned out to be a brand new, ex-works 9F, presumably on a running-in turn. As 9Fs were in any case almost unheard of in the Trent Valley at that time, this was definitely the cop of the day. If memory serves, it was 92015.

Often when setting off for a morning at the trackside, the aim was to be there in time to see the north-bound London–Barrow–Workington which passed Rugeley at around ten o'clock on its journey to the Cumbrian Coast. Motive power varied somewhat, which made it all the more interesting. The

named expresses were a folklore in themselves: The Royal Scot, The Shamrock, The Red Rose, The Mancunian, The Emerald Isle Express. Their very names invoked feelings of stability, excitement and a touch of mystery—a curious mixture. One wondered if they brought the same feelings to the lucky people who travelled in them. Amid a general aura of make-do-and-mend in those hard years following the war, the crack expresses did look the part, with well-groomed locos and coaches. BR's staff certainly made an effort where, arguably, it mattered most. The combination of a polished green steam locomotive and crimson-and-cream coaching stock, topped off with destination and train name boards, was unforgettable. And what a contrast with the lesser services!

The other end of the scale were the loose-coupled goods, usually in the charge of a 4F or a Super D. The Super Ds were representatives of the last ex-LNWR design still in use in the mid-fifties. Several of the class were shedded at Stafford, so they were in active use along the Trent Valley, including shunting in the yard at Rugeley TV. Their invariably grimy state was just one of their endearing features. They coughed and wheezed their way along in a ponderous yet determined way, refusing to heed the persistent and noisy protests of equally ancient wagons among the long rake in tow. Although at the time the Super Ds were the subject of not a little scorn and derision—they were usually dismissed as crates—it was easy enough to forgive coughing and wheezing from such stately old-timers. They certainly had character. Perhaps that was the clue: they were almost human.

Bellamoor Bridge was not good for photography because the railway was straight and flat, but ideal in all other respects. Surrounded by green pasture and hedgerows, with the canal and a copse of trees close by, the overwhelming effect was always of peace and tranquillity. Civilisation was just half a mile away, but might just as well have been a hundred. A typical summer day would find the intrepid spotters sitting on the wooden lineside fence a hundred yards or so down the slope from the bridge, with notebooks

Crewe North-based Jubilee class 4–6–0 No 45737 Atlas *pauses at Atherstone station with the 11.45am Liverpool to Rugby service on 23 May 1961. The three-coach train is headed by a Mk1 BSO with two LMS types following. Although running under express lights here, the train ran as an ordinary passenger service between Liverpool and Crewe. Worthy of note are the LNWR gantry signal box, the lengthy barrow crossing and the original station buildings dating from 1847.*

The 'Duck 8', or 'Super D', was the stalwart of the freight services on the ex-LNWR lines. On 19 February 1960 No 49441 arrived with a train of mineral wagons and promptly set about propelling them over the hump into the up sidings alongside Nuneaton Trent Valley station. One third of the 60 locomotives allocated to Nuneaton at this time were of this 0–8–0 type. By the end of 1964 the last members of the class had been withdrawn.

at the ready. Discussions, even bets, were rife on what would be seen that afternoon. The sun shone, with barely a cloud in the sky. Colour light distant signals a few hundred yards away were persistently yellow. The down fast distant, sitting at ground level in the 'six-foot' between the fast and slow lines, twinkled like a star in the heat shimmer above those ribbons of steel stretching almost to the horizon. There was no sound apart from one or two birds singing, and the rumble of a distant lorry. Without being noticed at first, the light changed to green. Experience suggested that there could still be a ten or fifteen minute wait before curiosity and anticipation would be satisfied, and today would be no exception. Would it be a Coronation, a Jubilee, a Patriot? Bets were on the larger power, as the Mid-Day Scot was due.

In the heat of the day, attention would wander, and that colour light had been green for what seemed like an eternity. Then, just as a grudging acceptance was about to take root that it was a false alarm—not uncommon—senses were re-awakened by a long shrill whistle. The rails began to sing. Yet there was still no sight of loco or train. The overbridge ensured that, but heightened the excitement and anticipation. Just as a pounding became audible, white billowing clouds of steam appeared against the sky beyond the bridge. Suddenly the void under the arch filled with the unmistakable face of a Coronation Pacific, bearing down on the expectant onlookers with relentless ferocity. For a mere fraction of a second the volcanic outpourings from the double chimney were prevented from heading skywards by the bridge itself, accentuating the blast of the exhaust. All of a sudden the locomotive became an aural and visual assault of four-cylinder music, giant drivers spinning like Catherine wheels, oscillating valve-gear. Then came the roaring waves as sets of bogies passed, their rhythmic clickety-click at a nearby rail-joint disturbed only by the passage of one of those elegant

Stanier twelve-wheel restaurant cars near the middle of the fifteen-coach rake.

Almost as quickly as it had appeared, the train was receding, as if too fast for its own flickering tail lamp to keep up. The white plume of steam became just a wisp on the horizon as the express rushed on towards Colwich and beyond. The stillness of the surrounding countryside returned.

Sometimes, for a change, a walk was undertaken beneath the tracks at the southern end of Rugeley Trent Valley station, and up on the bank where the line was in cutting. This provided a good vantage point directly opposite Rugeley No 1 signal box, where the Walsall branch diverged. The branch added an extra dimension, with the regular toing and froing of the branch passenger local, usually in the charge of a Stanier or Fairburn 2–6–4T, punctuated by less regular trains of coal empties setting forth on the long climb to Hednesford and the Cannock Chase collieries.

All the senses were vital to the train-spotter. The unique whiff of coal smoke mixed with hot oil and moisture was usually only momentary on the main line, but lingered compellingly in the confines of larger stations. The aural stimulus was often the more important, though, not only by emphasising the atmosphere that was uniquely railway, but also by encouraging curiosity. A rumble, a whistle, a clanking of buffers, the characteristic clonk as points moved or a signal cleared. All could give vital clues as to the form the next train would take.

Rugeley TV possessed a magnificent array of upper quadrant semaphores, including at the north end of the station, imposing double arm signals protecting the up lines. The settings of these signals often allowed a fair

Derby station still retained its overall roof when recently built. BR standard class 5 No 73002, of Derby shed (17A), was recorded leaving with a northbound local train in 1952. Part of the lattice footbridge that led across the south end of the station to the shed can be seen below the signal gantry to the left of the locomotive.

An hour at Dudley. Between the arrival of the single-coach auto-train, hauled by 0–6–0PT No 6418, from Old Hill at 6.18pm and the departure of the local for Walsall at 7.20pm in charge of Ivatt 2–6–2T No 41224 hundreds of passengers made the station very busy. Dudley Zoo was then a major tourist attraction and special trains were a regular occurrence. On 14 August 1956 Castle class 4–6–0 No 7005 Lamphey Castle *added a touch of colour to the otherwise drab scene, whilst at the north end Nos 42945 (6B), 42754 (16A) and 73046 (15C) left with return excursions to Leicester and other East Midland stations. No 7005 was renamed* Sir Edward Elgar *in August 1957 to commemorate the centenary of his birth.*

guess at the type of train due. Single-pegged on the up slow usually meant a loose-coupled freight, possibly the pick-up. Double-pegged on the up fast meant an express, or maybe a parcels or fitted freight. Single-pegged on the bracket for the fast-to-slow crossover almost certainly heralded the local from Stafford, making sedate progress along the Trent Valley while most other trains just passed it by. Travelling behind a 2P 4–4–0 in one of the old LMS compartment coaches was many people's gateway to the world.

What of other Midland train-spotting locations? Memories of Leicester Central are of a rather depressing, dismal station despite its elevated position. What activity there was consisted mainly of freight trains, rumbling through the station on to that long sequence of girder bridges spanning roads, shops and the rest of human activity in Leicester, from which the line seemed strangely detached. Maybe that was a major factor in its subsequent demise. But for the spotter the Great Central could be quite cosmopolitan: passenger trains were usually in the charge of Black Fives, whereas freights benefited from a variety of power, often of LNER origin. One such was 63777, an O1 2–8–0, which drifted through the station on the goods loop, its smoke dissipating lazily to join that from the chimneys of Victorian houses and factories dominating the murky Leicester skyline.

Derby was altogether more lively, and made the more interesting by loco shed and junction status. Lines seemed to emanate in all directions: Sheffield and Manchester, Nottingham and Lincoln, Leicester and London, Burton-on-Trent and Birmingham, Uttoxeter and Crewe. On one visit, 53807 (a Somerset & Dorset Fowler 7F 2–8–0) was in the shed yard, and

Director class 4–4–0 No 62667 *Somme* made an appearance on the Lincoln service—definitely high spots of the day.

The differences between the styles of loco design between the Big Four companies were fascinating and compelling. Visits to Wolverhampton Low Level or Birmingham Snow Hill were like entering different worlds for the products of Swindon Works were certainly distinctive in both sight and sound. It was not just the copper-capped chimneys, brass safety valve covers, inside valve-gear and cast number plates, but also cylinder shape, tender design, and a host of other features less easy to define. There was a degree of admiration for them even then by spotters with an LMS-based upbringing.

But ex-LNER locos were no less fascinating, so Peterborough was a haven in its own way. A4s presented an unforgettable spectacle starting heavy north-bound trains after their scheduled stops. Much fire and brimstone as, seemingly, most of the contents of the firebox and boiler were lost to the

The ex-Great Central line was renowned for its fast mineral trains hauled by ex-LNER class V2 2–6–2s or the newly introduced BR class 9F 2–10–0 locomotives. Enthusiasts who remember them thundering over the bridge across the LMS main line at Rugby will never forget the sight, or sound. No 92014 is seen passing Charwelton with a down 'Windcutter' on 19 September 1964. The locomotive is coupled to a high capacity BR1F type tender.

Lincolnshire atmosphere amidst spinning drivers and three-cylinder explosions. The A4s may have been sleek and fast, but they were also light on their feet. To be fair though, the ex-LMS Princess Coronations could have similar problems; on one occasion at Stafford, one of these superb Pacifics had great difficulty maintaining grip when starting a London-bound train, albeit of no less than seventeen bogies. Back on the East Coast main line, the other ex-LNER Pacifics seemed more sure-footed, and just as elegant in their individual ways. Added to these were B1s, B17s, V2s, 9Fs, WDs and a C12 (the Peterborough 4–4–2T station pilot) which appeared regularly there—a guaranteed feast of delights.

Back in those halcyon carefree days it was all too easy to become complacent. Steam ruled, had indeed done so since the beginning of railways, so the idea that change was inevitable, and indeed just around the corner, was not something that came to mind. Yet it should have been obvious, for on most days at Rugeley a foretaste of things to come was presented in sight and sound in the form of one of the prototype diesels, ex-LMS, ex-SR, or Deltic, doing the work of beloved steam locomotives which by then were having their last great fling. Perhaps it was all just a lingering dream.

BRITISH TRANSPORT COMMISSION
BRITISH RAILWAYS
LONDON MIDLAND REGION

B.R. 32735

YOUR REFERENCE

OUR REFERENCE

Telephone—

Telegrams—

....19......

Dear Sir,

VISITS TO MOTIVE POWER DEPOTS

With reference to your application for permission to visit Motive Power premises ; if you will kindly let me have the following information (giving at least 28 days' notice) by returning this form completed, I shall be pleased to give consideration to your application :—

1. No. of persons in party...........................
   (Permits cannot be granted to females)

2. Are you a male person over 21 years of age?............... If not, state your age.................
   (Persons under 16 years of age cannot be included in the permit unless in charge of an adult)

3. Give the ages of any members of the party under 16 years...

4. Is each member of the proposed party of British Nationality?..
   (Particulars of each individual to be given if an alien)

5. Depots it is desired to visit   6. Proposed date of visit   7. Proposed time of visit
   (In order of preference)

   ....

   ....

N.B.—Visits cannot be arranged on Saturdays, Mondays, or on the days immediately before or after Bank Holidays.

Yours faithfully,

....

....

....

Railway holidays very often commenced with the completion of this form. Hopes were always high that the application would be granted but very often requests to visit the busiest sheds would be declined.

18
NORTH EASTERN

VARIED indeed have been the celebrations, great and small, railway-oriented and about the comings and goings of the great and famous, at York station. But perhaps no informal gathering of the top management brass on the platform in the curved train shed had more poignancy than that on the first day of the 1948 summer timetable when the first postwar non-stop Flying Scotsman from King's Cross to Edinburgh passed through.

For a start the officials were proud of the fact that under the newly-established state ownership the North East had been granted its independence, the North Eastern Region, one of six, being the only English one to be governed from outside London. York was not just the obvious place for the Region's

headquarters, but for any major railway institution outside London (the railway museum was indeed just down the road). At Grouping in 1923 there had been considerable disappointment that not only had the North Eastern Railway lost its independence but the new LNER had not thought it fit to set up its entire headquarters here. The announcement in 1947 that British Railways were to have a separate

Scarborough was the North Eastern Region's largest holiday destination and even in the 1960s handled numerous extra trains during the summer season. In this 1965 view, a York-based class B1 4–6–0 No 61319 pulls a train of empty stock into the station ready to embark returning holidaymakers. A DMU service, no doubt highlighted in the timetable, stands in the next platform.

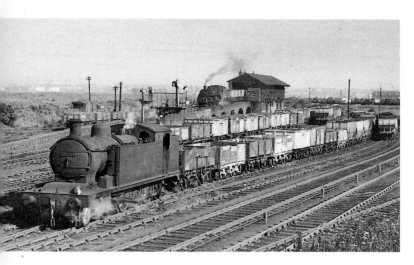

Coal was king in the North East and large mineral hauling engines were built in quantity to cope with this lucrative traffic. Fifteen class T1 4–8–0 tanks were constructed by the NER and later LNER to marshall the endless stream of wagons arriving at the North-Eastern ports. By the time this picture was taken, at Tyne Dock on 19 August 1960, No 69921 (an LNER-built example) was the sole survivor. A BR class 3 2–6–0 No 77014 shunts wagons on the coaling plant in the background.

North Eastern Region (and the tribute paid to LNER's policy of decentralisation that made it possible) was greeted with glee. Between January and July in this first year of nationalisation, tangerine paint had already been applied to numerous stations to emphasise new freedom and raise local pride.

It was a pride whose depth only those who came closely in touch with it can appreciate. Not only had the North East given railways to Britain and the world, but the North Eastern Railway, directly descended from the Stockton & Darlington, was among Britain's top three before Grouping—and far and away the LNER's best constituent. Despite the dreadful days of the Depression when the North East's heavy industry especially suffered, something of the enterprising spirit had been maintained under LNER ownership. There was, for example, pioneer resignalling at Leeds, Hull and Northallerton. The top brass of the new Region note the progress being made on York's own vast signalling installation, started before the war but only now being completed.

While they wait, the officials informally review a number of policy matters, perhaps talking of locomotives as railwaymen of this era ever did. Over a thou-sand pre-1923 locomotives built by the North Eastern Railway are still in service! Talk is always based on the need of providing a public service. Elsewhere nationalisation has been criticised for creating a monopoly; here, however, there has virtually always been one. You could indeed say that York station is an edifice to monopoly. Not only did the North Eastern Railway suffer much less competition than any other major pre-1923 company, but who could possibly have been more enterprising in the desire to serve the community and add to business? Where else were businessmen given such encouragement to leave their families at the sea for a month or more while they commuted at speed and in comfort back to the office? Were not even stationmasters encouraged to set up the selling of coal to supplement their wages? And where, during good days and bad, including LNER wartime ones, would you find branch line train services better geared to their traffic and the community needs; or provincial businessmen so early and so well provided with electric suburban trains at Newcastle? But oh for more modern, powerful locomotives.

And here, announced by the chime whistle of the A4, comes the first Flying Scotsman of the postwar era not to serve anywhere on the North Eastern (Railway or now Region). There is of course a down as well as an up side to that, but acceleration spells improvement, and that is what the management of this new Region stands for. The crews of preceding trains and signalmen will be aware of the need to clear the track to keep the non-stop wheels moving. The North East is proud to be independent, but insular it is not.

Heaton (52B) allocated Gresley class A3 4–6–2 No 60077 The White Knight crosses onto the North Eastern line for Harrogate and the North at Wortley Junction. It is leaving Leeds in the late afternoon with a Liverpool–Newcastle express in 1956 or '57. The change from London Midland to North Eastern Region motive power will have taken place at Leeds City, where the train reversed.

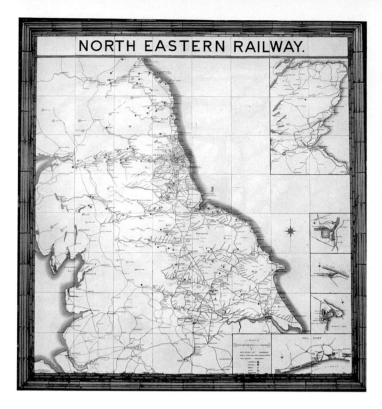

NORTH EASTERN RAILWAY.

North Eastern Railway tile maps were displayed at many of the company's larger stations. This one can still be seen at Saltburn station. Note the inclusion of the GNSR system in the top right-hand corner.

Because of flood damage to bridges further north, soon during this summer of 1948 the Flying Scotsman is diverted from Tweedmouth to St Boswells on the Waverley route. When a few drivers manage to keep the wheels moving, that makes the world's longest non-stop steam run of 408.6 miles. The branch is one whose management is arbitrarily cut in half: North Eastern to the border and then Scottish. But the North East gained from a relatively stable territory (there were more take-overs, especially in Leeds and Bradford, which became exclusive North Eastern territory, than losses) and undoubtedly that helps. Altogether there was less internal bleeding caused by management changes than in any other Region, helping the North Eastern to be cited as an example of how nationalisation should be.

Expresses become more frequent and heavier (though it took ten years of peace) faster. Apart from the ports-to-ports Newcastle to Swansea service via the Great Central, virtually all pre-war expresses were retained and many new ones added. The North Eastern Region's timetable, running to over 350 pages, proudly displayed the growing number of

named as well as by today's standard extraordinary range of cross-country services in its preliminary pages. The Queen of Scots Pullman went from King's Cross to Glasgow via Harrogate, while the Tees–Tyne Pullman served Darlington and Newcastle, the Yorkshire Pullman Bradford and Harrogate, and Harrogate still enjoyed its élite Sunday Pullman. The Flying Scotsman, Talisman, Heart of Midlothian, Northumbrian, Tynesider (sleeper), Scarborough Flyer (summer weekends only), North Briton (Leeds–Glasgow), the list goes on. Leeds and Bradford saw the West Riding and White Rose, Thames–Clyde and Waverley from St Pancras, and Bradford the South Yorkshireman from Marylebone. The Devonian for Paignton started at Bradford and called at Leeds. Every one of them, apart from the sleeper, had a full restaurant car.

Through trains worked by two routes to Bournemouth, and at summer weekends you could still catch a through train from Newcastle to Swansea via Birmingham or Rugby and Swindon, travel to a wide range of West Country destinations by night or day or come back from Ireland by through trains from Holyhead to Leeds to Stranraer to Newcastle. The coast route through Sunderland hosted many through trains, and nobody was surprised that on summer Saturdays you could travel by through train to Blackpool from places such as Salburn and South Shields, while destinations of trains leaving Scarborough on Saturday morning and afternoon sounded like a British geography lesson.

From Withernsea northward the railway served an incredibly varied range of resorts, and plain ugly colliery villages and ports: Hornsea, Filey with its triangular lead into Butlin's terminal station, Robin Hood's Bay and on perhaps the most romantic of all English seaside railways to Whitby with its Town and West Cliff stations, Loftus, Blyth and Newbiggin. The whole system including gems like Denby Dale, Oxenhope, Bolton Abbey, Richmond, Middleton-in-Teesdale, Alston, Alnwick was ours to explore for a week for £5 at the end of the 1950s. The North Eastern was given priority in the allocation of diesel multiple units and the Region was the first and most consistent in putting D at the top of the timetable columns. Many people who disliked the dirty local steam trains turned to the diesels and enjoyed the view forward and backward, especially on the scenic routes. Competition for the front seats was often intense.

But on the main lines steam remained almost unchallenged in the 1950s, the A4s doing yeoman frontline service, the non-stop through the Region now being the Elizabethan, King's Cross 9.30am, Edinburgh Waverley at 4.50pm. The number of long-distance passengers was greatly up from pre-war days, by a factor of ten on some routes, and though there were fewer slow-moving freights the East Coast main line was kept busy 24 hours a day—night services including a battery of lengthy sleepers which between them provided convenient journeys between scores of pairs of stations. From Newcastle in summer you could now even take your car while you slept to Dover, Exeter and Inverness.

The last years of the 1950s and the first couple of the 1960s indeed seem a golden age. When we look back through our rose-tinted memory, when even along the bracing North Sea coast the sun was surely ever shining on scantily-clad crowds on the beach, we have to admit that by this time not everything was well. Most of the nation's groceries were already going by road and, where it was not already the case, it was clear that the railway was going to be left with unremunerative odds and ends. Still a common carrier, the railway could not reject business... even traffic that never actually rode the rails. So once a week in the summer of 1958 a Walls ice cream van was seen delivering ice cream to Hexham station for delivery to outlying villages. The driver paid the parcels office a pittance on a mileage basis, and the parcels clerk paid out six times as much to a taxi to do the rounds. It could not last for ever.

Meat, fish, whisky and other staples of the East Coast main line were increasingly being lost despite the running of new express vacuum-fitted freights. On the passenger side, there had already been a considerable thinning out of branch lines, Pickering no longer being a railway crossroads, and much of the once-dense system to the west of the East Coast main line from Northallerton to Morpeth swept away... and more likely to follow. But the number of visitors arriving by train at Bridlington, Filey and Scarborough did not peak until around 1960, and faster, more numerous and heavier expresses were still the order of the day... veritable revolution being wrought on the East Coast main line with the intro-duction of the Deltic diesels in 1961. Gateshead

The non-stop, 9.30am Waverley–King's Cross, Elizabethan express runs through Newcastle Central circa 1959 headed by an A4 Pacific fitted with a corridor tender, to allow a crew change en route, and a double chimney. The colour light resignalling was completed by this date and so the distinctive bridge signal box, No 1, was redundant.

This busy country junction scene, showing a brace of NER class J21 0–6–0s working at Kirkby Stephen East station, was photographed around 1950. No 65038 has brought in a passenger train from Tebay, a service which ceased on 1 December 1952; it will make a connection with a Penrith–Darlington train. Meanwhile No 65090 appears to be engaged on shunting duties. Note the large amount of mineral traffic, which the cross-country Stainmore route had been built to exploit.

shared in their allocation with London and Edinburgh. Soon there were nine daily Anglo-Scottish trains and Newcastle was brought within 3½ hours of King's Cross.

Our enjoyment of those days was perhaps enhanced by the fact that the railway was becoming more passenger orientated, and while there were great innovations and accelerations tradition remained strong. The railways of North Eastern England had little more in common with those of, say, Wales than France, local practice and colour often enthralling railway-minded visitors from elsewhere. Images that immediately come to mind are of

returning excursion trains backing into the platforms at Scarborough, a great gantry for testing drivers' eyesight on the line to Blyth (where the dialect was so strong that an enthusiast could not understand the answer to a simple railway question), aged electric sets dashing in and out of Newcastle two ways to Whitley Bay, some of the nation's most stunning upland scenery en route to Middleton-in-Teesdale or Alston, and some of the most putrid coast between West Hartlepool and Sunderland where sea and coal and growing dereliction made looking out of the windows sheer Hell. There were still docks where coal trains dumped their prodigious loads, Pullmans on which smart Yorkshire businessmen knew they were entitled to the best, and usually got it... and everlasting level crossings whose gates you could see opening ahead of the multiple units, sharing the driver's view ahead.

Soon a great deal of it was to be lost, including the North East's own Region, albeit that the 1967 merger with the Eastern was based on York. But that is another story.

19
EVENTIDE

The evening sun is already casting long shadows in the valley below where the crossing station on the branch to the western coast has the neatness of a model railway. As the family picnic proceeds on the brow of the heather-clad hill, the sea visible one way and the valley and mountains beyond the other, the station is indeed like an untended model railway, all its signals at danger, a few trucks arranged in the compact goods yard as though for visual impression. It stays like that all day Sunday (except for an occasional excursion or track-maintenance train) and for long intervals during weekdays, too, but does suddenly come to life. Attractive though the coast is, some of us (the males!) cannot take our eyes off the railway. We might be hard pressed to analyse its attraction, for the charm lies in its totality: the picturesque setting, neat layout... and occasional bursts of movement between long siestas.

The first evidence of life tonight is audible, the distinct, clear whistle of a Great Western locomotive whose driver is announcing he is approaching the home signal and would like it off. Immediately we realise that a cross is going to take place, but it is early for the up goods (the day's only remaining timetabled train) and anyway it would be most unusual for the day's last down passenger to be checked by a freight.

The home signal drops after the driver has given a more prolonged blast on the whistle, and a green Prairie tank hauling a GWR standard non-corridor branch line set of two coaches and a parcels van emerges from the cutting and drifts into the down platform. Only the signalman is there to greet it, snatching the loop of the token and retreating hastily up the steps to his box. Two passengers, a mother and her boy of about seven, alight from the front compartment, the mother being dragged by the boy as he sees the signalman pulling levers in the box. Running down the steps the signalman pauses momentarily to collect their tickets before running over and then along the track toward the sea to the automatic token exchanger. The levers pulled included that for the up distant, only lowered when a non-stop train is going to make an automatic exchange.

We gaze at the train in the down platform, its guard talking to the driver. The little boy has now dragged his mother beyond the front of the Prairie tank and looks expectantly toward the sea for the non-stop train. After three or four minutes, during which the layout has again looked like a static model railway with human figures on mini-pedestals hidden from our view, it is clear that the up is not the freight mysteriously running early and given extraordinary priority but an express.

First we hear a distant barking of a steam locomotive against a stiff gradient and then we see billowing smoke and steam... and gradually two clear barks and two fountains of smoke emerge as the train swings round the curve and has a clear run through the up platform. Another Prairie tank is piloting a Mogul, both giving their everything though still all-to-well below the speed limit of 40mph through the facing point with nine packed assorted carriages behind.

Though the sun has just dropped behind the hill, it remains warm and nearly all the windows are open, young heads poking through half a dozen or so. The little boy waves to each of the drivers in turn, and we see the train engine fireman show his driver the token before hanging it up on its hook. It must be a return excursion, perhaps 400 people returning to we do not know what city after a sunny day on the sands.

First the engines and then the coaches disappear into the cutting, but the exhausts blasting out the chimneys still echo around the valley as the signalman returns to his box with the token left on the automatic exchanger and 45 seconds later comes out with it to talk to the driver of the delayed down passenger. There is no sign of passengers on that; they might be out of view in corner seats, but certainly did not come out onto the platform. Experience tells there might be a dozen at most, and this cross is a reminder that country and seaside railways often carry more passengers on one special than a whole day's ordinary trains, Mondays to Fridays anyway.

Tonight is Friday, and the big day when nearly a score of trains, almost twice the Monday to Friday quota, pass through this station in each direction is tomorrow. Normally all passengers stop here, but not on summer

Manor at sunset over the river Wye near Brachney. On 17 October 1964, just a few days before its withdrawal, GWR Manor class 4–6–0 No 7815 Fritwell Manor returns to Gloucester with an evening freight from Hereford. The passenger service was also steam hauled, usually by a Collett goods 0–6–0, Prairie tank or Mogul and remained in the hands of GWR motive power to the last day, 31 October 1964.

Saturdays when the automatic token exchangers come into their own. But the only hint that tonight is Friday is the parcels van behind the standard two-coach branch line set: PLA, no doubt. For the uninitiated, PLA is Passengers' Luggage in Advance. It will be delivered to hotels and boarding houses and be waiting in the bedrooms of tomorrow's arriving guests much as passengers on cruises find their luggage in their cabins.

At last mother has persuaded the boy to walk home and we see them climb up the hill toward us. They have nearly reached us when the signalman again walks to the automatic exchanger, this time no doubt for the goods, the last train of the day, and normally the only one using the exchanger except on summer Saturdays. Mother and son greet us and nearly pass over the brow of the hill when we tell each other that 'Here she comes'. Mother realises that's that and pauses to talk while the lad asks if we saw the special with its two engines and is this the goods?

It is. Its 0–6–0 tender engine can be heard for miles around as it lifts about a score of trucks up from sea level through our station to the summit several miles ahead. Why the line is kept open for the goods, or rather why the goods cannot run earlier, within the time necessary to open the signalboxes to cope with the passenger traffic, is anybody's guess; maybe it is so profitable that a bit of extra expense does not matter, or maybe the junction's marshalling yard could not handle it earlier. One thing is for certain: it has run at this time for generations rather than decades, balanced by an early morning down goods. That also is meant to run non-stop, but the automatic exchangers are seldom used since the box ahead is not opened early enough to allow the signalman to clear the signals and get to the exchanger in time.

In the gathering dusk the signalman returns to his box for the last time, there no doubt to wait ten minutes for the train to pass out of the section and to close down for the night. Mother and son finish their conversation with us, female and male respectively, and we wave as we ourselves begin to pack. The railway dead, our attention is now freely given to the shimmering sea.

20
EATING EN ROUTE

Princess Royal class Pacific No 46210 Lady Patricia *climbs Shap with a heavy northbound express in spring 1949. A Stanier twelve-wheel first-class restaurant car (the LMS preferred 'dining car' prior to 1946) is placed fourth in the rake and the third-class open vehicle immediately in front of it will probably provide third-class dining facilities. Both engine and train are still in LMS colours.*

OF all the pleasures of railway travel, none beat having a meal in the restaurant car. Who did not feel the better, refreshed, more knowledgeable, better balanced, as the result of a good breakfast or just afternoon tea at speed?

Was it that we were always hungry? Or that we had little other experience of being treated with such respect? Or that we could see a wider spectrum of the countryside from the 'open' vehicle than in our own compartment? Or that we met interesting people? Or, indeed, that walking down the corridor on hearing 'Take your seats for second lunch' provided a refreshing change?

All of these came into it, yet somehow the total was more than the aggregate of the ingredients. You became immersed in the total enthralling experience, exhilarated that you ate good food with excellent service at speed through the ever-absorbing countryside, and yet took this exhilaration in your stride as though having a fish *and* meat course, and moving the glass away from the cutlery to stop the rattle, were the most normal things in the world. Part of the fun might indeed have been that you took for granted

A Stanier third-class restaurant car No M138M stands in Euston station during the late 1950s forming part of a London to Manchester train. These massive twelve-wheel cars, built during the 1930s, weighed 50 percent more than a standard corridor third design. Note the proportions of smoking and non-smoking seating—times have certainly changed in that regard. This coach was withdrawn at the end of 1962.

much detail that many elders not used to eating at speed found distinctly novel. Many did not instantly comprehend the basic mechanics of the menu.

To which it has to be added that those able to take full meals were privileged. Excellent value though they might be, they were always expensive and beyond the means of many. You felt especially privileged sitting with glass in hand at the window when a train ran into a busy platform and those waiting opposite cursed their luck that they had positioned themselves where they could not get on.

Because of the expense of main meals, and especially the agony of having to do with a Plain Breakfast while others around you devoured their fry-ups, we often had to take our own sandwiches but treated ourselves to morning coffee or afternoon tea. They were not to be despised, for (apart from perhaps the issuing of a meal ticket) their serving involved all the elaborate procedure of the restaurant car: going there at the right time, perhaps just ahead of the official call, choosing an ideal facing window seat. You were served by a battery of waiters, asked politely if you wished more tea or coffee and then (as an individual bill was written) whether everything had been satisfactory. You were thanked for the tip—and stayed seated enjoying the ambience and the better view until it was obvious your presence was no longer welcome.

When funds allowed, what thrill it was to walk down the outside of the train at its starting station to request a meal ticket from the steward standing with packs in hand (one pack for each sitting) by the car door. Why was it always the 'car'? Down the train the steward would refer to the car as though every other vehicle was something different. The cars were often fascinating, frequently more venerable than the rest of the train. You might indeed be lucky enough to be served on a vehicle with six-wheeled bogies or be in the third class car separated by an entire kitchen car from the first class one of an LMS dining trio. Or take afternoon tea beside Loch Awe on the way to Oban in a former Pullman redolent of yesterday's luxury. Or enjoy a Gresley catering vehicle long after all others of his vintage had gone to the scrap heap. But you wanted to avoid being trapped in the windowless Bulleid tavern cars of the postwar Southern. Generally seating was more comfortable in restaurant cars than ordinary coaches, you were free from the nuisance of other people's luggage, and—as today—you were often seated first class when paying first-class fares was out of the question.

Part of the excitement was that generally you ate by the clock. On some Highland routes you had to take an early meal one way, and a late one the other, since the same car served down and up trains, its shunting from one to the other always adding interest. But even if you and the car made the entire journey, sittings were fixed according to traffic demands and staff convenience. Everlastingly there was pressure to serve you early, but where possible you waited for the last sitting, noticing when passengers from the previous one started drifting back to their seats.

Food was undoubtedly important, and usually (especially for those more likely to splurge on a meal on the move than one in an hotel) it spelt a reasonable degree of luxury. Immediately after the war menus were thin, the emphasis on chicken and tinned plums, but by the mid-1950s older passengers said the fare was as good as ever. Where else did you get such a breakfast plate, fish as well as meat at lunch and dinner, and so elaborate an afternoon tea? And what decisions! Fresh buttered toast or toasted tea cake? Dessert or savoury of a kind you would never find in any other eating place you patronised? After a pudding had been set down three times and the request for savoury repeated yet again, the parson opposite said that one would go through life a lot more easily conforming. Why?

Restaurant cars were not the place in which to be nobody. Better to be wicked, like dithering so longingly over the choice between buttered toast and tea cake that the steward gave you both, or to ask for cheese (always accompanied by celery the like of which again we never saw elsewhere) after pudding... or savoury after cheese. When the chief steward commented 'You like your savouries, sir' you felt really someone... and were relieved when you were not charged for the extra course. All of which perhaps does less than justice to the main courses. Meats and fishes were excellent, steak and kidney pies, for example, baked on the train with thick, crisp pastry and oodles of meat. Another touch of magic was that whereas at home and in most cafés and restaurants used in ordinary life vegetables were heaped on the plate, here you could decide which you wanted and which you could happily do without. While the peas were being chased round the bowl, you perhaps asked which was the train's balancing working, and so showed your interest in the railway and might later be told titbits of information, possibly about next summer's timetable.

Perhaps the best journeys of all were those on which one had successive meals at the same seat served by the same friendly crew. That was living. While conversation in the compartment was rare and when it happened often boring, only the more interesting people seemed to make it to the restaurant car and here exchanging views and information was ever welcome. To be told that one's company had been so enjoyed that could

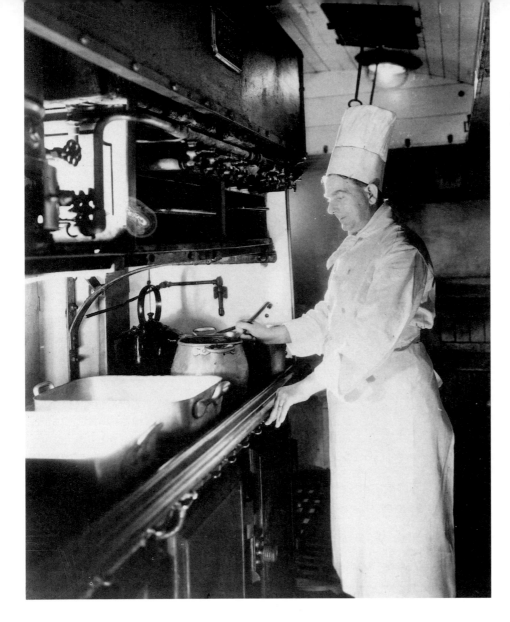

one's bill be paid for was both flattering and made another restaurant car meal possible when funds were tight. Usually, of course, they were. Back home people who had never had the experience sympathised with us for having to make do with railway food, while we knew we were giving ourselves a special treat. (The fact that Dad treated himself but not the rest of the family to lunch on a 1930s Birkenhead–Kent express is still resented over half a century later. But one thing you rarely had to suffer in the car was the nuisance of other people's children.)

Over the years there was much fraternity with the stewards, as witnessed between them and guards, ticket collectors and those ladies who on the trains we loved went backward and forward making sure toilets were clean. Whether or not the restaurant were the only 'car', it was certainly the heart of the train... the place you visited for hot water or to warm baby's milk or even a bandage. The press made fun of the fact that a lonely American visiting Britain at the time of the Festival of Britain curtailed his exploring when he found friendship and comfort in the restaurant car to Hereford. He spent the rest of his vacation going to and fro, taking all his daily meals on board, merely filling in time during the London stopover. We understood.

21
SCOTTISH

FOR the Sassenach alighting north of the border for the first time, Glasgow is a wondrous place. The journey has been exhilarating, including lunch over Shap and afternoon tea climbing Beattock. The timetable has told us there are four termini, three with large railway hotels attached to them, and we know there is an independent underground nicknamed the Clockwork Orange, and that Glasgow is

An up freight hauled by domeless class 5 4–6–0 No 45168 crosses the bleak landscape near Dalwhinnie on the Highland line in 1955. The snow fences are to protect the line at this exposed location. The composition of the train gives an indication of the variety of traffic still being handled at this time.

the last stronghold of trams. But nothing prepares us for the pleasures in store.

It is still light when we roll across the Clyde into Central on a summer's evening a few years into nationalisation. There is no hurry to leave the station since we have a room in an outlying hotel booked and have been told what tram to take. We are amazed at the scale of activity on the sloping concourse. We have never seen anything like Central, with many of its platforms perpetually used by two trains at once and the massive display of details of departing trains, each train given a large placard put into its appropriate window by men who can be seen checking the

paperwork and making occasional telephone calls to ensure they get it right. At any one time there are a hundred people looking up at the display, while others continuously passing by glance up for confirmation they are going the right way. Each of the 13 platforms has its large, individual slot, so if there are two trains they are both included on the moveable placard with a clear 'Front' or 'Rear Train' before the list of stations served. To the left is space for special announcements and details of the expected punctuality or otherwise of long-distance arrivals, of which there are remarkably few. The whole display, occupying an entire floor above the restaurant, formerly general waiting room, is topped by 'Train Information' displayed in magnificent lettering. To the right of the restaurant, timetables are displayed and prove endlessly interesting.

Here is a truly major station but with only a handful of services for England. Most are going to places whose character we can only guess at... and many of which we have not even heard. The Cathcart Circle sounds so intriguing that we decide to put it high up on our priority list for the following days. But then the names of places to which there will be a steamer connection to from the Gourock express

The last Pacific locomotive built by the LNER, class A2 No 60525 A. H. Peppercorn passes Ferryhill Junction as it leaves Aberdeen with the up West Coast Postal service for Euston on Saturday 16 June 1962. The passenger coaches at the rear form a Glasgow service. Eleven members of the class, which totalled fifteen in all, were based in the Scottish Region.

sound as if they are straight out of a novel. We are amazed there even is a Gourock express, a full-length train with a 2–6–4T displaying express headlamps... and that soon there will be another, from the platforms furthest from that at which we arrived.

There is a wide roadway before these last two platforms serving the Gourock expresses and trains for Wemyss Bay and we walk down it, beyond the extensive glazed area and find a short platform which on an old plan is labelled the 'Fish, Fruit and Milk Platform'. From its end we can see everything coming and going. The sound of wheels hardly ceases, and when momentarily it does you can hear the points constantly being changed. Often three, four or even five trains can be seen moving at once if you look back into the glazed station, for it takes a minute for a short train nearest the buffers to emerge onto the bridge over the Clyde. Everything is steam,

with some new BR Standard class tanks mixed with LMS and older machines some of whose like we have never seen before. Few would win marks for cleanliness. Much of the rolling stock is also pretty grotty, and trains on some routes seem very lightly loaded. Noting our interest in the last stages of the rush hour, the drivers of some of the light engines coming off one train, pausing shortly in a siding on the bridge, and backing onto a new arrival, wave their hands. These light engine movements are smartly made.

Walking back to the concourse, we note that the angle between the buffer stops of different pairs of tracks is at roughly 45 degrees to the station front. That and the slope, and the fact that every inch of the site surrounded by streets has been used to the full while giving an impression of spaciousness, make Central a real one-off.

An Edinburgh Waverley station pilot, class J83 0–6–0T No 68481, pauses for water in the early evening sunshine at the west end of the station. Six of these former Holmes, North British Railway tanks were painted lined black in recognition of their high profile duties at Waverley.

The world speed record holder for steam, class A4 4–6–2 No 60022 Mallard, *passes through Portobello c1958 with the prestigious East Coast non-stop service between London and Edinburgh The Elizabethan. The performance of the immaculately presented A4s on this service was keenly observed and recorded by both railwaymen and enthusiasts alike. The weight of the train, often over 400 tons, made this 6½ hour journey in many ways a much more exacting working than the pre-war Coronation, with formation weighing 312 tons tare.*

Overleaf above **Jersey Lily**
The Great Central main line out of Marylebone was the last major trunk route to be built in Britain and provided fast services from the capital to the east Midlands. J.G. Robinson's beautiful class 8B Atlantics worked the top expresses into the twenties and thirties and were considered by many to be the most elegant machines ever to ride the rails. Hence their popular nickname 'Jersey Lily', after the heart-throb actress of the time Lily Langtry. No 1086 in all her glory is seen here at Neasden engine sheds flanked by a pair of pom-pom 0–6–0s. When the GC was absorbed into the London & North Eastern Railway, much to the disgust of GC fans, many of these Atlantics were painted in plain black livery, and their shapely Robinson chimneys exchanged for a less flattering variety.

145

Above **North Western Style**

The London & North Western Railway made its locomotives earn their living and often hung loads on the drawbar that would have made other companies wince. It was also the first company to utilise water troughs and eventually had nine sets along the main line between Euston and Carlisle. Here, on Bushey troughs, a Precursor 4–4–0 No 1419 Tamerlane takes water while heading a heavy Euston to Manchester express in the early twenties. This engine was designed by George Whale and built at Crewe in March 1904, superheated in 1913 and eventually withdrawn from service by the London, Midland & Scottish Railway in March 1936. One hundred and thirty of these excellent machines were built up until August 1907. They typified the 'Premier Line's' locomotive design of the period.

Opposite below **North Eastern Elegance**

The North Eastern Railway was, in many ways, the most substantial constituent of the LNER. The locomotive designs by Sir Vincent Raven provided substantial motive power. His handsome Z-class Atlantics were introduced from 1911 and operated express services over the North Eastern section of the East Coast main line until superseded by the Gresley Pacifics from the late twenties. No 2201 is seen making a thunderous departure from Darlington just prior to the grouping of 1923.

We are back early in the morning by one of the newer bogie trams to see the rush hour arrivals in full flow, and then visit the other termini in turn. The main upper level at Queen Street is again full of character even though the air is smoke laden and we do not want to linger at the tunnel end, however enjoyable the sound of an express leaving full blast with the aid of a banker. The acrid atmosphere in Low Level makes one glad that London's underground was long since electrified. When two trains leave at once, you can hardly see people on the opposite platform. There is talk of electrification here and welcome no doubt it would be. Meanwhile people seem a bit thin on the ground and most trains unnecessarily long. A huge number of stations are however

The competition between the North British and the Caledonian Railways in Edinburgh left an impressive legacy of station buildings and hotels at opposite ends of Princes Street. The Caledonian station, named after that splendid thoroughfare, is seen here with a BR standard class 5 4–6–0 No 73056 departing with an ordinary passenger service for Carstairs and Lanark c1956/7. Both station sign and locomotive numberplate are backed by the Scottish Region's light blue colour scheme. Princes Street station closed on 6 September 1965.

served from here, including even Balloch Pier when there is a Loch Lomond steamer to connect with.

It is good to be in the clean surroundings of the underground, officially the Glasgow District Subway, and delightful that such ancient equipment (you can see clearly into the control room) still earns its keep. The two-car train, all original stuff, slows as it comes up the slope and stops at the narrow island platform. All stations are at the top of slopes for this was once a cable railway. We feel as though we are in a movie, but the locals take it for granted.

We alight at St Enoch, and admire the subway's own above-ground station building, which would perhaps be more in keeping as a decorative eating place in a public park, before being lured up the slope to St Enoch, always referred to as St Enoch's, fronted by a truly massive hotel. The station concourse enclosed in almost a half circle of glass is something else again. It is all pretty gloomy inside, the booking office almost church-like. At the platform's end, out in daylight, we hear an LMS Class 2P 4–4–0 come screeching in. Trains are mainly local, though sometimes several are lined up beside each other at the ten-platform terminus. After a walk round the city, we come back to see the rush hour and see off the

5.30pm with its through coach for Plymouth, due 2.25pm tomorrow, but decide not to wait for the Thames–Clyde Express which takes exactly ten hours to get here.

Like most visitors who allocate Glasgow a few days, we sample the joys of the Clyde (which means taking a boat train to Gourock down quadruple track to Paisley, and some fast running) and unlike most of them try a suburban route or two, in one case out by train and back by tram. Pretty grim! The fourth terminus, Buchanan Street, is left till we depart for Oban and discover it is not much more than a slum, though it does have very interesting trains. Our Oban journey is going to be a real eye opener, the first of dozens along those great scenic single lines with sparse services but full-length trains with restaurant cars that are such a feature of the Highlands.

The details of that trip are not for here. What was obvious is that Scotland was different in everything, including its city stations as well as its scenery. Geography was a major factor, but so, too, was population. Glasgow, Britain's second largest city, was enormous and of course still is; today Glasgow accounts for over a third of ScotRail. But while roughly two-fifths of Britain in land area, Scotland accounted for only ten percent of the population. The visitor could be excused for having the first impression that the whole of the rest of the country was a playground for Glasgow and to a lesser extent Edinburgh and other Central Belt folk. Certainly nowhere in the world were better touring facilities by public transport available than from Glasgow.

Yet Scotland's premier railway, the Caledonian, had earned the most profitable part of its keep from coal and other heavy traffic, while coal had also been vital to the Glasgow & South Western and the North British. And how they fought for the coal traffic and any other, including commuters, that was going. Much of the density of the Glasgow suburban system was due to competition. But then the Scottish companies found it hard to stop competing even where there was not much to compete for. It just seemed a Scottish characteristic. The other two major pre-1923 companies, the excellent little Great North of Scotland Railway, and the much more spread out Highland Railway from just north of Perth to Wick and Thurso, even had their colourful spats.

The Grouping era had brought two very different

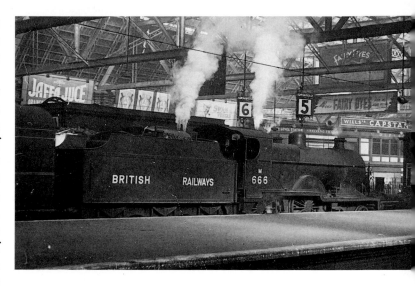

LMS class 2P 4–4–0 No M666 stands at the buffer stops of Glasgow Central's platform No 5 on 24 April 1948. The engine is plain black and displays the post nationalisation interim livery markings and numbering system. Note the large arrivals and departures board in the background.

styles. The LNER delegated, and the GNoS, mainly beyond LMS rails through Aberdeen, had continued with considerable independence, albeit benefiting from more powerful locomotives. The LMS in its emphasis on standardisation had swept away many of the Scottish companies' locomotive classes, almost entirely abolishing those of the Glasgow & South Western, and seemed to wish to abandon any special Scottishness of its operations north of the border, though to the working railwaymen, geography and tradition were not easily beaten by Euston's paperwork. The LNER's attention to detail was infinitely better than that of the LMS though, notwithstanding showpieces such as Edinburgh Waverley and the Forth Bridge, the infrastructure inherited from the Caley was superior to that the North British bequeathed the LNER.

Both LMS and LNER poured scant resources into their best Anglo-Scottish expresses. Never before had the difference between the unbeatable best and the appalling locals of the industrial areas been greater. The Coronation Scot and Coronation. What memories they evoke! How proud we were to catch a glimpse of either or talk to someone who had actually been on board. In truth very few people patronised them, both because of the limited accommodation and the shortness of the trains' lives. Never again

Pacific Parade

The country end of platform 10 at King's Cross was a mecca for train watchers from nine to ninety, generation after generation gathering to witness spectacles such as this. The period is the mid-fifties as a Gresley A4 takes off with the Tees–Tyne Pullman whilst a Peppercorn A1 No 60131 Osprey *waits to follow on with an express for Leeds and Bradford. Locomotives had to work particularly hard out of King's Cross up the steep gradient through Gasworks and Copenhagen tunnels. The cacophony was music to the ears of platform-enders. The A4 depicted here No 60015* Quicksilver *did not survive the cutter's torch but happily five sister engines did. All of the A1s were scrapped but at the time of writing there are plans afoot to construct a brand new engine from the original blueprints. What an achievement that would be.*

were we to see such luxury on British rails secured simply by paying for a ticket, albeit including a supplement.

However, express trains generally improved dramatically during the Grouping years, in a way that by and large locals did not. And at nationalisation, when Scotland was given its own Region, it was obvious that those foundations would be built upon as soon as better times returned.

Scottish joy at having its independence was considerable, but while the North Eastern Region was poised to take instant advantage of York's regained freedom, north of the border there was an inevitably painful merger between the former LMS and LNER interests. Schisms went deep... from top managerial level to the men on the ground. Hardly anyone was satisfied. Though the first chief regional officer was an LNER man living in Edinburgh's North British Hotel who hardly set an example—not merely by refusing to move to the new Glasgow headquarters but doing the daily journey from railhead to railhead in a chauffeured car; at first it looked as though LMS interests might win. But one by one other former LNER men took key posts, and ultimately the LMS inheritance was considerably less treasured than the LNER one, though both suffered enormously.

This is not the place to recount the story of the especially severe Beeching cuts in Scotland and the closure of the LMS road to Aberdeen. The trains we loved mercifully ran ahead of that period of disaster, from which it has to be said the Scottish Region did eventually emerge with its own unified style and commercial drive... but that is even further in the future so far as we are concerned. We did enjoy the short-lived initial success of the Glasgow blue electrics, most starting on 5 November 1960. Traffic shot up in a gala atmosphere reminiscent of line openings of Victorian days, but next month we heard with horror that they had had to be withdrawn for technical reasons and all the old steam locomotives and their rolling stock brought back—for what turned out to be a painful ten months.

The Scotland we loved, while nearly everything was still steam, saw steadily accelerating expresses, freight as well as passenger. Innovations included the popular cheap-price Starlight Expresses from Marylebone to Edinburgh (Waverley) and St Pancras to Glasgow St Enoch (eventually as many as half a dozen packed trains a night), car-carrying sleepers

and observation cars on the great scenic routes. The number of day and night trains from London by East and West Coast routes was far greater than before the war, while internally the Glasgow–Aberdeen service (including three top named restaurant car trains) combined comfort, style, speed and reliability... ultimately with Gresley's A4 Pacifics when they were replaced by the Deltics on top-line duties on the East Coast from London.

All this, and hardly anything had been lost. The excursion programme, especially from Glasgow, was as generous as ever, with numerous combined train/bus/ship services. The Waverley remained the pride of the North British's 'other' main line, from Carlisle to Edinburgh, while the famous Thames–Clyde Express also from St Pancras still served the G&SWR route from Carlisle to Glasgow. Though actually in England, Carlisle was one of the most colourful of 'Scottish' stations, with two main lines from the south and three to the north, plus the Port Road to Stranraer (an early casualty but then still carrying the nightly sleeper for Northern Irish passengers) and the cross-country line to Newcastle and the ex-LNER branch to Silloth.

Glasgow and its environs could warrant a fortnight's holiday if you let it. Edinburgh Waverley was one of the most marvellous of places, and if you ever needed a change you could sit in Princes Gardens watching the everlasting stream of expresses, locals and freights pass out of the tunnel and along the quadrupled track into the station. Perth was another joy, a real crossroads with endearing touches such as its own range of expresses to and from Euston, early car-carrying trains, heavy Post Office business and a frontier atmosphere, for everything going north of here seemed to linger to gain strength before setting off. It was not as varied especially in carriage livery as in earlier time, but in the course of a few hours you seemed to cop the very oldest and the very newest that BR had to offer. That included short pick-up goods that clearly were not going to survive much longer and some of the new vacuum-braked freights which gave a greater impression of permanence than later experience justified.

Of the lesser junctions, Crianlarich always springs to mind. In fact it was hardly a junction, for only after the introduction of diesel multiple units did one offer a day trip from Glasgow to Oban coming down the West Highland and switching to the former Caley

West Highland-based K2 2–6–0 No 61788 Loch Rannoch *eases out of Fort William yard during shunting operations c1952. Its home shed (63D) can be seen in the background. All the K2s transferred to Scotland received side window cabs and in addition 13 locomotives were named after lochs close to the West Highland line.*

road here. The ex-Caley one-platform Crianlarich (Lower) was deemed one of the least important calls on the old Callander & Oban, romantic a route though it was in total. But the West Highland's island platform reached by underground passage and including (as it still does) a tea room attracted anyone with the slightest railway interest passing through by car, while if you were a train traveller you dashed off to make the best of the ten-minute refreshment stop in the days that the restaurant car only served full meals.

And the branch lines! Not merely were all the great scenic routes open, but many sprouted enthralling branches. Changing from the Oban train to either Killin (its locomotive shed in a dead end a mile beyond the station at Loch Tay), where shunting was normally by gravity, or Ballachulish perhaps was only

a touch less exotic than taking the Light Railway from the Mound to Dornoch. You needed to immerse yourself in the timetable to make the best of scant connections, and even to understand the basic geography of the GNoS's connections at Cairnie Junction (like Killin Junction only an exchange platform without road access). In the reverse direction, you could say farewell to a friend as the train was divided into two parts at Elgin, and get together as it was joined up again 70 minutes later. The Coast line gave gorgeous views of fishing ports and resorts, but

St Margarets Sunset

Edward Thompson's B1 4–6–0s were intended as the LNER's 'go anywhere', 'do anything' mixed traffic locomotives and eventually totalled 410 engines built between 1942 and 1950. They replaced several life-expired 4–6–0s and 4–4–0s from all of the constituent LNER companies. One of the named members of the class, No 61244 Strang Steel, *is seen in the golden glow of the evening sun in the shed yard at St Margarets depot, Edinburgh, in the early sixties. This painting was created from notes and photographs taken on several visits to the depot in steam days. 61244 was a St Margarets inmate. For many years the artist pondered the meaning of this odd name until he discovered that Mr Steel had been a director of the LNER.*

the restaurant car went by equally attractive distillery country. Taking the train across Buchan brought the joy of passing one or more fish trains heading for England (unless there had been a storm) and fitting in the brief ride on from Fraserburgh (with its neat terminus with wooden booking hall) along the sands to St Combs. Every train to St Combs had its locomotive fitted with a cowcatcher. While you could see a much smaller percentage of Scotland's than England's coast from the train, there were other great stretches, on the main line to Aberdeen built on the cliffs with bridges over frequent gullies, and at several points on the North line but especially at Brora.

Fixing itineraries took so much time that we tried to do it before leaving England. We enjoyed the timetable footnote saying a train would stop to uplift passengers if timeous notice were given, but found we had not properly understood another footnote, or find that there was a cheap offer locally for a circuit we had thought would be too expensive. The type of trains and scenery, time, money, food, overnight accommodation all had to be taken into account. When we could afford it, we delighted in the first class freedom of Scotland ticket, whatever it was then called. Even cheap day tickets had their first-class version… though good use could be made of the new single second-class sleeper cabin from King's Cross to Edinburgh which alas did not last long.

We were always treated with great civility by staff and other local people… and not infrequently invited into signalboxes or onto footplates. It was sad to see traffic on lesser routes drop away sharply after the first few seasons of nationalisation, though even when the public had largely deserted the former GNoS branches it was still enjoyable enough meeting other enthusiasts who seemed to provide most of the traffic.

The greatest thrill was arriving on an overnight train from the South at Edinburgh, Glasgow, Perth, Aberdeen, Stirling or Inverness (we never made it on the once-weekly sleeper to Oban, and the West Highland was altogether too special to sleep on) and seeing the different landscape, the single-storey cottages and crofts, and sniffing the sharper air. You can still do it… indeed still alight on the platform and pick wild raspberries and roses while waiting to cross a train in the opposite direction—and who should discourage today's travellers from making the most of what is left? Yet in our hearts we know we were privileged to enjoy the very best days when steam was just one of the links deep back into history, when every station had its smiling staff waiting to please, and we were taking the most adventurous journeys any of our family or friends had yet even contemplated.

There was, of course, a down side. Some things, like restaurant car meals, tended not to be so good north of the border. Once Springburn had supplied not only much of Scotland but the world with its locomotives from the four great works crowded into a square mile of Glasgow suburb. Decline there was early, and sadly Cowlairs works came to have a poor reputation for the quality of its maintenance work, though this (and the contrast in quality provided between it and the ex-LNER works) became more evident in diesel days. Perfection you seldom had. Few of us complained about the overall picture in the 1950s.

This map is reproduced from the reverse of a Holiday Runabout ticket for Area No 18. Issued at Elgin on 1 July 1957 it was valid for one week and cost £1 third class. In fact third class had officially become second the year before.

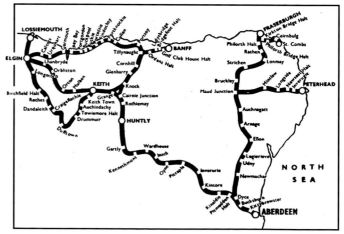

22
AUTUMN

If there is a steady time of year on the railway, it is the autumn. First the state and then private schools are back, the winter timetable is in operation, freight business is buoyant and at least for the next couple of months there is little chance of a major weather-related catastrophe. If punctuality is not good now, it never will be.

As the steam-heating season begins, many passenger trains shed a coach: it is commonly stated that heating uses as much steam as carrying the extra load. There is little overcrowding and at most junctions trains are arriving embarrassingly early; if only this quality of journey could have been offered at the end of July and beginning of August. Restaurant car crews however look forward to brisk business. This is their busiest or at least most rewarding time of year as the captains of industry do much of their annual business travel and well-to-do provincials go to London for a show and to shop. The Motor Show and other exhibitions stimulate business, culminating in the Fat Stock Show at Smithfield. From much of Britain that provides restaurant cars with their largest wine bills accompanied by the year's most generous tips.

Workers' trains are running like clockwork (embankments even of electrified lines are mowed by hand so there are few trees shedding problem leaves), and early closing days see many towns sending large contingents to the nearest city for entertainment and shopping. It is all just as it should be: cosy, efficient, lacking in high drama but still varied. Saturday-only last down trains on branch lines become the busiest of the week. But in some cases that is because there is not a comparable bus. The writing is alas on the wall for many branch lines. Indeed, from even before nationalisation the last day of the summer service has seen the last trains on more lines, but it is still only those that can never have paid their way that are yet threatened.

Let us say it is 1954, and on the freight side optimism is almost total. 'On British Railways, improved recruitment of traffic staff, better wagon availability and turnaround, and adequate engine supply should go far, with improvements such as a more extensive use of alternative routes for goods trains and reorganisation of marshalling yards, to ensure smooth freight working.' The yard master invites a reporter from the local paper to see for himself. Freight trains are running longer distances without stops and serving more destinations without remarshalling. Typically a city of 250,000 people despatches a freight every 45 minutes from mid-evening until breakfast time, with about half that level of activity during the day. Though groceries are increasingly being delivered by their manufacturers' C-license lorries, overall business is still increasing to record levels. The forecast total traffic is 180,000,000 tons, nearly 2,500,000 more than last year.

Overleaf above
Fighting Duchess
Beattock Bank in Dumfriesshire has been immortalised over the years by the work of many fine photographers gracing the railway press. Among the best was the late Bill Anderson whose wonderfully lit shots taken at this location certainly made an impression on the artist. The year is 1938 and Princess Coronation Pacific No 6232 Duchess of Montrose *is virtually brand new. She is seen tackling the gradient near Greskine with a fifteen coach express helped in the rear by a 2–6–4 tank from Beattock. The crisp and even snow is interrupted only by the orderly footprints of a lineman who has disappeared into the distance. By many observers Stanier's Duchesses in this form were considered to be the pinnacle of British steam locomotive design both in appearance and performance. They were certainly handsome machines.*

157

Opposite below **Scotch Goods**
Freight traffic, or goods as it was then known, was the life-blood of most railway companies. This was especially so for the London & North Eastern Railway. The express service from London to Scotland, the 'Scotch Goods' as it was popularly known, was a fine example of commercial acumen being served by dedicated staff. Worked by top-link engines, including Pacifics in later years, the goods was timed to express schedules. The Gresley V2 No 4774 is almost brand new as she sets out from King's Cross yard with the express goods in 1937. The Great Northern, like many railways of the day, was well blessed with attractive lattice-post signals and the imposing example here provides balance to the composition.

Above **Waiting in the Night**
There is something intoxicating about railways at night—especially with steam locomotives. The artist has vivid memories of lying in bed as a child and watching the orange firebox glow, and leaping sparks dancing to and fro past his bedroom window, the crew silhouetted against the glare with the fireman hard at work with his shovel. Surely many 'old masters' would have had a field day with such an evocative subject. Here, at Washwood Heath yards, Birmingham, a Stanier 8F No 48197 waits for the road not long before the end of steam in this area.

159

Ancient and Modern. Dean Goods 0–6–0 No 2411 turns south off the Great Western main line at Thingley Junction with a Swindon to Westbury freight in 1952. In the background the second Western Region gas turbine locomotive, built by Metropolitan Vickers, No 18100 heads the up Merchant Venturer for Paddington.

Carrying that calls for dedication and much unsociable work. Drivers and firemen of freights as well as passenger expresses are still subject to double-home working, and though more trains are partially 'fitted' (with vacuum brakes) guards have to alight from their vans at Stop Boards to pin conventional brakes down, the locomotive then pulling the trains down hill against the force of the brakes which have to be picked up at the foot of inclines. Some people say British Rail should have gone in for Continental-style bogie goods vehicles, but the rigid-based 4-wheeler is preferred for its cheapness and flexibility. Well over 50,000 of them are being built this year. Each hundred or so yards of street effectively owns several coal trucks.

Coal stocks are being built up for the winter, and the railway has won some business that used to go by coastal steamer, which proved unreliable in the 1947–8 winter. The yard master quotes other facts. Steel, that necessity of modern Britain, is on the up and needs another 3,000 trucks this year. Locomotives are more powerful, morale good because wages are higher and some weekend work has been curtailed. This yard which in LMS days used to work continuously is now twice the size but closes at lunch on Saturday till the early hours of Monday morning. That helps recruitment. Before the war everyone wanted to be a railwayman but now it is more difficult.

Traffic buoyancy is reflected down the branch line. Coal is the universal staple but each route has its specialities. Cement and quarry stone are on the up over much of upland Britain, sugar beet in East Anglia, teasels in Somerset, fruit from Kent and the West Country (who can forget the smell of the Tamar Valley strawberry specials?). Early Saturday morning hop pickers' specials from London to Kent are still great social events, and the hops they pick along with those from Herefordshire pour into Burton-on-

An up express freight, with loaded cattle wagons marshalled behind the locomotive, passes Charfield on the Midland main line from Bristol in the early 1950s. Motive power is provided by class 5 2–6–0 No 42872 of Derby shed (17A); its tender still carries LMS markings.

Trent, to be carried again as spent hops. Snape Maltings at Aldeburgh are not yet devoted to music but served by several trains a day at this time of year. Barley is being delivered to the Highland distilleries. Milk having to travel more than a hundred miles almost universally goes by train, as do horses. Lambourn and Newmarket head the places where a supply of horse-boxes is always on hand; in the mid-1950s up to a thousand new horseboxes are being built annually, the Western Region sticking to its own design. Scores of cattle trains run from ports served by the Irish ferries and from the English shires. In Ireland itself probably more head of cattle and horses are on the move than human beings, certainly outside the big cities.

We stop for lunch at a pub by a country station in Herefordshire. While our parents see what is on the menu, we watch the arrival of the down freight, with fifteen trucks between Dean goods and GWR guard's van, the station truck in the middle which squeaks to a halt outside the parcels office. There is a kitchen mangle along with pieces of farm apparatus, canisters of liquid gas, and crates and boxes that reveal little except the desire to improve living standards. The railway is benefiting from the increase in mail order catalogue buying. 'Better be off on your way,' says the signalman when assured the engine does not need a drink, 'and drop what you have for us on your return. There's a couple of hops to make the real stuff for you to pick up then. The special's right behind.'

Parents come out of the pub to say it is too busy with cattle dealers but, on seeing that display of disappointment that only a boy about to be deprived of seeing his train can make, decide there is no hurry after all and they might as well enjoy the 'local colour'. Indeed, as the special with eighteen cattle wagons arrives behind a Prairie tank, a sandwich is delivered and commented on by cattle dealers coming to the station to do the paperwork of conveying their purchases to Birmingham or by farmers just come to use the lavatory. 'Better eat that up here,' says the signalman.

The footplate crew of the special also come to the box, for social exchange of no practical purpose, but give an invitation to join them running round the train. Three blasts on the whistle as we clear the points at the up end of the loop has several farmers jump at the cattle pens below the embankment where the auctioneer is intoning away. Before parents finally run out of patience passengers and parcels start arriving for the up passenger that will be the first of three trains following each other to civilisation. Parcels include several trays of mushrooms and a crate of rabbits, legs up. 'Used to be lots more before myxomatosis.'

In a strange city that night sleep is impeded by the constant banging of trucks in the marshalling yard and occasional whistling of locomotives. On a crisp, windless night, trains can probably be heard by two-thirds of Britain's population, though perhaps only four or five million as noisily as this. As autumn proceeds (half term giving a sharp one week boost to passenger business) another railway noise wakes people up: the fog signal. Autumn may begin smoothly, but seldom turns into winter without fog. If the wheels are slowed down, much of the blame no doubt rests with the railways themselves as thousands of locomotives pour soot into the atmosphere... often a score of them under Liverpool Street's roof alone and many more at other London termini and locomotive depots. You notice it even in Devon: the

morning sun brings golden hues to a village, but five miles away Newton Abbot with its locomotive depot and coal-fired electricity works has a miniature smog making it silly to wear a white shirt.

But even around London and in the industrial Midlands and North, fog is generally only a railway irritant rather than a crisis. Newspapers and mail are delivered on time and few office workers arrive late. Though only the Western has its Automatic Train Control, rear-end collisions in bad visibility are rare, that at Harrow & Wealdstone in 1952 being exceptional in its consequences—a double collision killing well over 100 people, and giving impetus for an improved nationwide ATC.

Autumn ends on 21 December with the Christmas rush. Though it is not usually said of autumn, it comes in like a lamb and goes out like a lion, traffic being busiest when days are shortest and the weather most fickle.

The Southwell 'Paddy' pull-and-push service awaits the right away on its last 2½-mile journey to Rolleston Junction with the 8.30pm train on Saturday 13 June 1959. From Monday 15 June the service was withdrawn. Last days' of service and line closures were soon to become a common feature of every change of timetable, with many occurring with the introduction of the winter service in September.

23
TO BEYOND MIDDLETON TOP

IT was that doyen of branch line photography, Arthur 'Cam' Camwell, who clinched the matter. 'North London tanks? Of course they are still at it!' What he meant was that these veterans, even in the early 1950s, were still double heading just half-a-dozen goods wagons up the steepest incline in the country, the 1 in 14 at Hopton between Middleton Top and Parsley Hay—two magnificent Derbyshire names to get your tongue round—every working day. And, to make matters even more interesting the very last LNWR 'Chopper' 2–4–0 tank was 'at it' too, working the short level section between Sheep Pasture Top and Middleton Bottom. Rather like an animal at a safari park, No 6428 was trapped on the section. It could only escape by being lowered down or hauled up a rope-worked incline.

In the mid-twentieth century the Cromford & High Peak line was certainly an anachronism. But then it was so even ninety or so years earlier, when it was acquired by the London & North Western Railway. The original intention was to link the Cromford and Peak Forest Canals by the High Peak Junction Canal from Cromford to Chapel Milton. The route via Grindleford, Hope and Edale, which included a tunnel 2¾ miles long, was surveyed by John Rennie in 1810, but failed due to great expense.

A more practicable alternative (but only just!) was a railway. The Cromford & High Peak Railway was incorporated by Act of Parliament on

The Cromford & High Peak line was a quaint survival into the 1960s having two rope-worked inclines and the steepest adhesion bank in the country—Hopton, 1 in 20 steepening to 1 in 14. In the early 1930s some ex-North London Railway 0–6–0Ts were drafted in to replace ageing LNWR 2–4–0Ts. LMS No 27527 was the Cromford Wharf shunter and is seen at the foot of Sheep Pasture Incline c1947. Visible through the A6 road bridge is the catch pit built to derail runaway wagons.

One of the LNWR 2–4–0Ts survived into BR days as No 58092 and worked the isolated section between the two rope-worked inclines Sheep Pasture (top) and Middleton (bottom). It finally succumbed in 1952 when it was replaced by LMS class 0F 0–4–0ST No 47000. No 58092 is seen on this section shortly before withdrawal.

2 May 1825. The line was opened in two sections, from Cromford Canal to Hurdlow (foot of incline) on 29 May 1830 and on to Whaley Bridge on 6 July 1831.

There were nine inclines worked by endless chains powered by stationary beam engines built by The Butterley Company. Originally the sections between the inclines were worked by horses but locomotives were introduced in stages from 1833. A passenger service of sorts ran from 1833 until April 1876. It is not clear whether this was a horse drawn coach or locomotive worked, and the mind boggles at the thought of passenger coaches being worked up or down 1 in 8 gradients with a single chain the only saving link between life and death. The real traffic, however, was stone from the quarries along the route.

The C&HP was leased to the London & North Western Railway for 999 years in 1861, complete amalgamation coming in 1887. The Premier line had no other such oddity, but as narrow-gauge systems and other oddities, even the Liverpool overhead, closed it seemed an ever-stranger survival and attracted ever-more railway lovers. Some of the latter even travelled—standing up—by special train in London Midland Region days.

If one started at Cromford and climbed north westwards, the first leg meant using the inclined plane to Sheep Pasture at 1 in 9 then 1 in 8. By big railway times this formidable climb had become double track with steel cables replacing the old chain. Each 'run' of wagons, on balanced up and down workings, was attached by two chains. These had links as large as that of a standard link coupling at the end which was dropped over the drawhook of the leading wagon. From here the chain tapered, link by link, to a size little longer than an ordinary strong dog chain; it was wound round and

165

A few special passenger trains were run over the C&HP in the 1950s and early 1960s for the benefit of enthusiasts. The first was organised by the Stephenson Locomotive Society and Manchester Locomotive Society and ran on 25 April 1953. The special, headed by NLR 0–6–0Ts Nos 58860 and 58856, is seen at Middleton Top awaiting its passengers who had walked up Middleton Incline.

round the cable, the smallest link being tied by a leather thong. This involved a special railway trade classification: 'chain hanger on'.

Normally it was hard to get a ride but a programme made for the BBC worked wonders, even foolhardy wonders. Travelling up on the footplate of an old LNWR tender bound for the hamlet of Longville which was dependent on this sole supply of water, gave one cause for trepidation. Looking down at the deep catchpit for runaways laid between the tracks at the bottom, there were strong hopes that the 'chain hanger on' had made a secure job of it. Knowledge is sometimes inconveniently recalled! Such as that the pit had been placed there after a spectacular runaway in February 1888 when a brake van and a wagon of limestone had broken away at the top of the incline. After shooting through Cromford yard, beating any landspeed record of the time by a handsome margin, they took flight and in one huge leap they cleared two sidings, the Cromford canal, a farm road and the Midland main line. Peace of mind was not helped either by recalling that even in the mid-1950s the motive power on the next incline was still the old Butterley Company's beam engine installed when the line was built. This ride was by courtesy of a dismantled ex-LNWR 0–6–0 DX, installed in 1884.

At the top the old Chopper shunted wagons, trundling them several times a day to Middleton Bottom where the 'Cromford Experience' was re-enacted. The Butterley engine did its job quite happily.

At Middleton, more sidings; and, in the small shed, a couple of North London tanks. Cam was quite right. One of these ancients was still in LMS livery, the other in new gas-tarred black had British Railways emblazoned across her side tanks. One still carried the NLR bell-mouthed chimney, the other a tall LNWR one, a reminder of Crewe standardisation and owner-ship. A strange migration of old engines to this bare, treeless, stonewalled uplands of the Peak. From here on it was pure adhesion working but what a working, two engines running flat out on the first stretch to just make it over the top, sparks flying in true North Western style, setting fire to the grass by the 1 in 14 gradient post. It was quite an occasion—and well worth coming back the next day for pictures.

Middleton Top shed in its declining years when it was home to two class J94 0–6–0STs, which replaced the NLR locomotives. No 68012 stands in the remains of the shed building which lost its roof during a gale in 1962. On the road adjacent to the shed are a number of ex-LNWR tenders which conveyed water for locomotives and domestic use to strategic points along the line. The limestone countryside made water both scarce and unsuitable for locomotive use.

24
IRELAND

THE Great Northern is a grand railway. Its timetable highlights the twice-daily crack Enterprise Express running up the coast from Dublin to Belfast and the seasonal Bundoran Express winding its way up the border to the Atlantic rollers. Beyer Peacock of Manchester supplied 3-cylinder 4–4–0s for the first, and dainty inside-cylinder ones for the second. All have gleaming brass nameplates and a rich livery of sky blue and scarlet. The Enterprise Express is first and third class only, while others (apart from the one-class railcars) are still first, second and third. Typical of the attention paid to detail by the GN(I) on Saturday the Bundoran Express runs non-stop (70 minutes) from Dundalk to Clones, but on Mondays to Fridays makes a call each day at a different village to enable people to spend a few hours on the sands at the resort. The timetable also

The Tralee & Dingle Railway served the second most westerly railhead in Europe and were it not for the monthly cattle specials would have closed in 1947. These trains enabled the line to exist, just, for another six years by which time the locos and rolling stock were completely worn out. A double-headed empty cattle train hauled by 2–6–0Ts Nos 1T and 2T, built by the Hunslet Engine Company of Leeds in 1889, takes water at Anascaul in 1950. Both the locomotives were withdrawn in 1954.

lists dense suburban services at each end of the Dublin–Belfast line and sparse but well-organised services on remote branch lines; some call 'at certain Level Crossings on request'. One 'train' is but a single horse-drawn tram, from Fintona Junction to Fintona. Electric trams run up the Hill of Howth connecting with the Dublin suburban steam trains.

The tiny Dundalk, Newry & Greenore, built by the English London & North Western Railway to provide its Holyhead passengers with its own Irish port, is one of a number of minor systems unexpectedly surviving because it straddles the border and the two sides do not talk about the mounting losses. Included in the survival is the huge hotel and golf links at Greenore: you can lie in a cavernous bath with the window open inhaling a smell of Crewe steam, for three Victorian Webb 0–6–0 saddle tanks still keep going. Not only that, the original six-wheeled passenger stock is in daily use painted in LNWR plum and spilt milk.

The Belfast & County Down has green Baltic tanks to Bangor and 4–4–2 ones in a couple of sizes to Donaghadee. The newly nationalised lines of North and South have not yet had time to alter their liveries completely, so LMS red and Great Southern

Great Northern Railway (Ireland) three cylinder compound 4–4–0 No 83 Eagle *built by Beyer Peacock & Company of Gorton, Manchester in 1932 and withdrawn by the Ulster Transport Authority in 1960.* Eagle *carries a Belpaire boiler; the original was round top, and is painted in the glorious blue livery adopted by the GNR c1939.*

black/dark grey abound.

This is Ireland in 1949. One uses old railway ships to cross the Irish Sea. First class has plush dining rooms and there are a few cabins with beds and salt-water baths for a small supplement.

World War II has been over for nigh on four years but fuel restrictions have been severe until only months ago. Eire has but one commercial coal mine, its quality so poor that the stuff can only be used in power stations. Nationalisation will soon lead to rationalisation, so this is the time to have a last look at a scene which is, even now, a reminder of the good days.

There is much to attract. Derby built engines run on the former Northern Counties Committee (LMS) lines of the Six Counties (or 'Black North' as it can be called down south). Woolwich Moguls, inside-cylinder 4–4–0s, 0–6–0s and 2–4–0s, make up most

There was never very much through working between any of the Irish railways, but between 1950 and 1953 the GNR and CIE collaborated in a through train between Belfast and Cork named Enterprise—an extension of a purely GN train between Belfast and Dublin. The down train (from Dublin) is pictured at Amiens Street station Dublin, the GNR terminus, hauled by ex-Great Southern Railways' three cylinder 4–6–0 No 802 Tailte. In the background is GNR articulated diesel railcar 'G' on a train to Howth. This service is now electrified and the trains run through from Howth to Bray using the former City of Dublin Junction platform Nos 5 to 7.

of the motive power on the old Great Southern system, now Coras Iompair Eireann (CIE). And the last railway in the British Isles to have 'Great' in its title, the Great Northern, still justifies it. It straddles the border, dealing separately with two governments who do not recognise each other... but in a few years its mounting losses will make them talk together for the first time.

Another system which is already surviving on borrowed time because it also crosses the border is the creaking Sligo, Leitrim & Northern Counties Railways, whose 0–6–4 tanks are named but never numbered. It is one of Ireland's attractive oddities which of course include the narrow-gauge systems. These range from serious concerns like the County Donegal Railways, to the Tralee & Dingle, only coming alive when it is poked, which we will return to shortly.

Ireland is very much Ireland: class 3 roads are dirt, cars are few, you bump along the branch over short rails at a fastish lick in an old 'sax whaler' where the guard is a 'grand man' in pouring rain which is a 'foine soft day now'. Below the border chocolate is not rationed; you can actually find bananas and cream after a huge steak and the Guinness is superb. When the sun shines in the west the light is pure crystal. But do not be surprised when the kid across the aisle is sent to beg a sixpence.

To the English eye traffic outside the large towns

(which really means only Belfast and Londonderry, Dublin, Limerick and Cork) is sparse. But this is not just a sign of the times. It is a sensible part of the Irish way of life, for the largely agricultural community rarely moves beyond its village and market town. An absence of minerals makes railway freight traffic cling to this agricultural pattern. Many a station in rural areas has only one or at the most, two, train(s) in each direction daily, and arrival is something of an occasion, with news exchanged while parcels traffic is being bundled in and out of the van. Even such focal points as Mallow and Limerick Junction enjoy long spells of cloisteral quiet, broken by brief periods of frantic activity when the rare trains arrive, complete with vintage engine and heterogeneous stock, to make their elaborate inter-connections. Dublin's busiest stations, Amiens Street and Westland Row, compare naturally with London's Marylebone.

Checking the distances between stations on the major lines it becomes apparent that although a train may be booked to call at every one, the quality of the running is quite high and much better than the timetable might suggest. Low train mileage and the need for economy mean engines and stock have long

Cork Glanmire Road locomotive shed, probably in the early 1950s, when the CIE was still 100 percent steam. From left to right the locomotives are 342 class (D4) 4–4–0 No 346 built by the GSR in 1936 at Inchicore and withdrawn in 1960; 393 class (K1A) 2–6–0 No 394 (of SECR design) built by the GSR at Inchicore in 1930 with parts supplied by the Woolwich Arsenal, withdrawn in 1959; 60 class (D14) 4–4–0 No 60 built by the Great Southern & Western Railway at Inchicore in 1891 and rebuilt with Belpaire boiler in 1934, withdrawn in 1957; 101 class (J15) 0–6–0 No 241 built by the Great Southern & Western Railway at Inchicore in 1902 and retaining its original round-top boiler, withdrawn in 1957.

lives. In fact, apart from obvious LMS-built Moguls in the north, most date back to the old pre-1923 and 1925 companies. But this does not mean leaking, clanking engines in poor mechanical condition. Often, in performance and outward appearance, Irish steam puts its British counterpart to shame. Stand on the platform at Omagh and see the Great Northern's *Croagh Patrick* sweep in from Belfast like a well groomed horse, her immaculate livery reflecting in a symmetrical pattern the whorls made by the cleaner's cloth, and you cannot but be impressed. Above the magnificent coat of arms on her splasher, the brass nameplate flashes in the sun whilst cab and boiler fittings are spotless beyond reproach.

The Irish train can be equally magnificent, if comprising a motley collection of vehicles in shape, size and age. It is reminiscent of the LNWR. In fact the Great Southern has a North Western air about it, its engines all carrying Crewe-type cast number-plates. Within a decade change will become complete, today's occasional modern steel coach will be the norm, its elliptical roof and electric lighting

The London & North Western Railway owned the Dundalk, Newry & Greenore Railway in Co Louth and Co Down. It was a microcosm of the parent company. This photograph taken at Greenore about 1950 shows one of the six 0–6–0STs, No 3, which were Ramsbottom/Webb special tanks adapted for the 5ft 3in gauge and typical LNW signals. The whole system closed on 31 December 1951.

replacing the gaslit period interior of the elderly eight-wheeled clerestory or the jolting six-wheeler. The latter still populate the branches snaking along with no sprung seats and with the old pot-lamp holders still in place on the roof. These ancients, however, are well maintained and upholstered, exteriors newly painted and door handles polished. Passengers are few, in first class usually only the occasional priest.

The narrow gauge West Clare boasts a six-wheeled saloon still in Great Southern maroon with that company's coat of arms on the doors. The Donegal too has its saloons but these only come out on the occasion of the Bank Holiday steam specials to Ballyshannon.

With the exceptions of the new Ulster Transport Authority's (ex-NCC) Belfast–Londonderry, the Great Northern's Dublin–Belfast, and CIE's Dublin–Cork routes, there are few Irish lines which would not be considered to be very secondary in England, essential links though they provide. This is particularly true of the undulating single tracks that run across the Midland bogs towards the mountainous far west of Connaught or Kerry. There is an air of adventure that permeates these trains which two or three times a day set out over their long and usually lonely tracks. In his *Lines of Character*, L.T.C. Rolt calls them 'ships of the bogs' and the stations 'rare oases welcoming their coming'. Such thoughts slide easily through the mind when musing over the

journey in a well-stocked and comfortable dining car making the most of the wide loading gauge of the 5ft 3in track. On the longer branch lines in the south, one-time Great Southern & Western Class J15 0–6–0s introduced as early as 1866 vie with Midland Great Western 2–4–0s dating from 1880. Most of these lines, like the Valentia Harbour branch (the most westerly in Europe) are full of character. Virtually all such trains are mixed and slow. But who would be rushing when there is so much to enjoy? But do not take too much notice of the timetable broadsheets. Trains are worked to local advantage.

For example, the 3.06pm from Cahirciveen to Farranfore, leaves at 2.30. It gives people plenty of time to do their shopping at Killorglin. No notice of this appears of course; why should it? Dublin seems pretty nearly as remote and irrelevant as Paris so far as Kerry people are concerned.

The independent Sligo, Leitrim & Northern Counties, linking Enniskillen in the north with Sligo in the south, is a line of such decrepitude that only a personal ride over it can demonstrate. It defies adequate description. The daily mixed runs within an hour or so of time. It has one magnificent tri-composite coach. The first class seats are coming unstuffed in places, the lighting is intermittent. Yet two of the 0–6–4 tanks are modern, delivered in 1947 by Beyer Peacock notwithstanding the railway is in receivership. Investigation proves that they are being paid for on the never never. Maybe Beyer Peacock did not do a customer investigation before starting work and have not been paid? While passenger business even at the line's HQ, Manorhamilton, is light, many cattle pass through it. Handed over by CIE they are taken over by the GN (or GN(I) as it should be properly called) en route from cattle fairs in the south to the English market.

The continued independence of the lines crossing the border is fine for the enthusiast who can revel in the blue of the Great Northern, the geranium red of the County Donegal or the olive green of the Lough Swilly. The narrow-gauge railways are a fascinating group notwithstanding the Damoclesian sword which hangs over them all. They have no parallel whatever with any lines over the water. Once there were eighteen of them, all using the Irish sub-standard gauge of three feet with a total mileage of 562. Now there are seven, mostly the longer concerns which were built to serve the 'congested areas', a

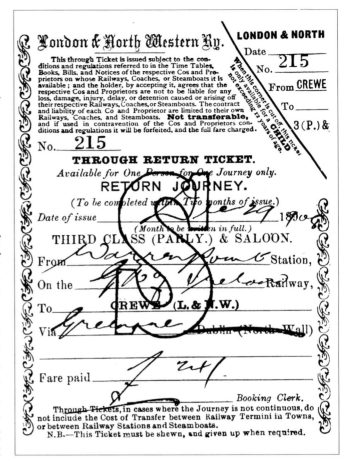

The return portion of a London & North Western Railway ticket permitting travel from Warrenpoint to Crewe via the steamer service from Greenore. Third class on the train and saloon (first class) on the boat, all for 24s (£1.20).

peculiar turn of the century phrase for the poor regions of the west with more population than resources to feed them.

The Tralee & Dingle Railway is special. Built on a shoestring to open up one of the poorest of Ireland's counties, the life of this remarkable piece of railway hangs by a very slender thread, its active locomotive power down to three 2–6–0 tanks which only come to life on the occasion of the monthly cattle fair at Dingle. On the Friday before the empty stock is worked down in one or two trains, depending on the season, returning fully loaded the following day. These trips are probably the last examples of adventurous railroading in the British Isles; they will cease when the road becomes paved. Of all the railways of Ireland the T&D retains its original character. The rails lie rusty, dulled by a month's disuse, only three platelayers service the thirty-one miles of track that cross the Slieve Mish mountain on grades of 1 in 30/31 and the guard is relegated to only a small section of his van which has been adapted to carry more cattle, a waist-high partition protecting him from too intimate an association with the livestock. On this line you forget London and Dublin and all the cities of the earth. Dingle is the gateway of an older and simpler world; from here it is but a little way by mountain road to Dunguin, the harbour for the Great Blasket where islanders speak of America as their next parish. The abounding memory is of the double-headed train behind 1T and 8T, the first and last 2-6-0 tanks built for the railway blasting their way up the Gelnagalt bank, chimneys erupting pillars of smoke in every way equal to those guiding the Israelites out of Egypt.

County Clare has a coastline swept by heavy gales, it is wild, stony and inhospitable to man, a fact quickly discovered by the Armada survivors wrecked on its shores. In many places the three-feet West Clare railway is fully exposed to Atlantic gales, their fury being such that the authorities installed an anemometer at Quilty station, and concrete blocks have been placed under the seats in the passenger stock to aid stability. This inhospitable coastline and stony inland terrain compete with a circuitous main line to make the West Clare's survival remarkable, but the railway still runs. It has no major traffic but takes everybody and everything that elsewhere now goes by road.

The narrow gauge uses a bay platform of the broad-gauge station at Ennis, its engines taking water from a tank beneath which is a gents lavatory, an economical arrangement. Leaving the yard the train runs eight miles north to Corofin, west through Ennistymon where they play the fiddle like an angel's song then over a 250ft summit to Lahinich, turning due south to follow the Atlantic for twenty-two miles to Moyasta Junction set in dreary marshlands, where the Kilrush and Kilkee tracks go their separate ways. By rail the journey to Kilrush is forty-eight miles, by road it is twenty-eight. And when the road is improved that will be it—though there are rumours of railcars to come. The West Clare engines are a mixed bag, 2-6-2, 0-6-2 and 4-6-0 tanks with outside frames.

The Cavan & Leitrim is a far cry from the West Clare. This piece of railway connects two townlets

The other English railway to own and operate lines in Ireland was the Midland and its successor the LMS. Again the Northern Counties Committee, as the Irish lines were known, reflected mainland practice. 2-6-0 No 100 Queen Elizabeth built at Belfast York Road in 1939 is seen at the head of an up express at Antrim in 1950. The coaches are LMS designs built c1934 for the North Atlantic Express service from Belfast to Portrush.

and two railways, Belturbet with the Great Northern and Dromod with the CIE. Its importance lies with the branch running from the railway's hub at Ballinamore to Arigna perched on top of the Bralieve Mountains and Ireland's only coalfield. Coal is lowered down from the mine to the railway by means of an aerial ropeway. This tramway-like branch, the last section of narrow gauge to be built in Ireland, dates from 1920. Because of its proximity to the public road, there is a (theoretical) speed limit of 12mph beyond Ballyduff.

It is a poverty-stricken countryside, stony and pitted with small lakes where cold grey rocks protrude like bones through the thin covering of soil. But the Cavan & Leitrim has its moments. A few years back, for example, there was a phenomenal avoidance on the Arigna branch near Drumshambo, the road criss-crossing it now and then causing some alarm to the local horse-drawn traffic. This time it was a motor car which failed to notice the train suddenly swinging from one side of the road to another. After the normal altercation, the police arrived, resulting in the engine driver, Patrick Rowley, being fined two pounds at Carrick on Shannon Court for giving insufficient warning of his approach.

A visit to Ballinamore shed requires old clothes as the environs seem to be covered with coal dust and

The Great Northern was unique in having steam, diesel and horse traction until 1957. (The line from Dublin to Howth was later electrified as part of the Dublin Area Rapid Transit, 'DART'.) The horse traction was the ¾ mile branch from Fintona Junction to Fintona in Co Tyrone. This was from opening in 1853 the terminus of the line from Londonderry (Londonderry & Enniskillen Railway) and was locomotive-worked. However this only lasted some seven months as the L&E main line was extended from the junction to Dromore in 1854. The passenger service to Fintona was then horse-worked until closure in 1957. The tram shown, GNR No 381, was built by the Metropolitan Railway Carriage & Wagon Co in 1883 and lasted until closure. The photograph was taken in 1950.

Three of the three-foot gauge lines inherited by the Great Southern Railways lasted until the 1950s, and the West Clare until 1961. The Cavan & Leitrim main line connected the MGW at Dromod with the GNR at Belturbet and the Arigna branch from the line's headquarters at Ballinamore served Ireland's only viable coal mine. For most of its length the Arigna branch was a roadside tramway and is seen here at an ungated crossing coming alongside the road in 1957. The locomotive is ex-Tralee & Dingle 2–6–0T No 3T built by the Hunslet Engine Company of Leeds in 1889 and transferred to the C&L in 1941 and lasted until closure of the C&L in 1959. The photograph was taken in the last couple of years of the line's life.

nothing, absolutely nothing, is ever cleaned. The locos and rolling stock, however, are pieces of Irish railway history; the original C&L 4–4–0 tanks have been augmented by 2–4–2 tanks from the erstwhile Cork, Blackrock & Passage Railway where they ran nippy suburban services and *all three* classes of engines from the Tralee & Dingle, a standard 2–6–0 tank No 3T, 2–6–0 tank No 4T (the small Kerr Stuart engine) and the infamous 2–6–2 tank No 5T which was wrecked with the runaway pig train at Glengalt. Add to this lot a curious set of coaches from old bus bodies to venerable eight-wheelers having clerestories and American-type balconies with gates in veranda rails.

Further north the two largest narrow-gauge systems are thriving and retrenching respectively. Owned jointly by the Great Northern and the successors of the English Midland Railway, the County Donegal Railways Joint Committee is very much alive. The credit here is due almost entirely to the introduction of railcars by the late Henry Forbes

(pronounced 'Forbess' on the railway) between the wars. This remarkable man also introduced a system of sealed containers loaded in Dublin by the Great Northern travelling in bond through the intervening Six Counties, being transhipped at Strabane to narrow-gauge flat trucks. Ingenuity and variety have kept this hundred and one mile gem of the narrow gauge going. With its railcars, including a veteran from the long closed Clogher Valley Railway in the North, the ten geranium red 2–6–4 and 4–6–4 tanks, all named, the CDRJC has an over-abundance of power to cover its passenger and freight services. Often special vans painted red are attached to the rolling rollicking railcars giving rapid parcels facilities, but freight is usually run by steam several times daily except beyond Stranorlar to the west where once a day suffices. The solely English-owned section from Londonderry to Strabane is one hundred percent steam.

A permit to ride in the van or on the engine of the daily mixed west from Stranorlar brings pure delight. Perhaps the engine is the 4–6–4T *Erne* or the 2–6–4T *Columbkille*, but whatever the motive power the train will be long and heavy, sweeping round on a great curve to face a continuous five mile grade of 1 in 60 into the Donegal highlands, a climb which keeps the fireman busy. The crew are probably the McMenamin brothers who have been on the job almost forever. Topping the summit the tracks parallel the edge of Lough Mourne, its steel waters ever troubled by the mountain winds. The mountains ahead seem to bar any further progress but a deep and narrow defile opens up whence the train drops down through the stark Barnesmore Gap, again at 1 in 60, the track clinging to precipitous slopes high above the floor of the pass. Down through Lough Eske with a view encompassing the Blue Stack Mountains and into lavishly-signalled Donegal station for a shunt before traversing the long winding extension to the deep waters of Killybegs.

The time to visit the Donegal system is the August Bank Holiday Monday, when steam passenger trains run from Strabane and Stranorlar taking town and village to the sea at Ballyshannon—or rather Bundoran, a good walk further on. The sight of these specials using every available piece of passenger rolling stock there is, wending their way home in the dusk high above the road through the Barnesmore Gap, is etched in the memory for a lifetime.

The Donegal and Lough Swilly systems meet across the road at Letterkenny. The Swilly's story is very different. Beautifully maintained dark green 4–6–2 and 4–6–0 tanks work the freights to Letterkenny and Buncrana, each with a slatted wooden-seated passenger brake van at the end. In the shed at Pennyburn, Londonderry, two huge 4–8–4 tanks slumber and at Letterkenny there is a 4–8–0 tender engine, once used for the wild and desolate extension to Burtonport, now closed and taken up. It was seventy-four miles this journey, entailing a spectacular climb to the far west out of Derry and the crossing of the Owencarrow river by a long viaduct. In 1925 a train was blown off it.

Handfuls of passengers, mostly shoppers from Pluck or Newtoncunningham use the unwelcoming compartments of the Lough Swilly brake van on the Letterkenny–Londonderry train. These freights are well loaded and shunt nearly everywhere. There is a box of butter here, a few empty coal wagons there and often a cattle van or two full of beef which get discharged pell mell onto the station platform. The railway runs through prosperous agricultural country and a great deal of general traffic is available including tons of potatoes. Soon it will all go by road.

After Newtoncunningham the line drops down along the shores of Lough Swilly, the driver closing the regulator and wiping his hands on a piece of oily waste; he leaves the job of braking entirely to the guard, explaining that he is a 'grand man'. As the train gathers momentum, and the swaying wagons behind seem disproportionately large for the ever narrowing track ahead, one loses faith for a second

until the screw brake takes effect and couplings tighten. Tooban Junction, a desolate island platform with a lonely signal box, is the crossing place for the down goods from Derry and the jumping off point for the Buncrana branch which still sees the odd passenger excursion at weekends and Bank Holidays. The border comes next with perfunctory customs examinations, then the workshops at Pennyburn seemingly full up with company buses and the dark gloomy Graving Dock terminus. What a railway it must have been in its prime.

In the north things are more prosaic, the Great Northern and the old NCC run into Londonderry linking it with Dublin and Belfast, though off the Derry to Belfast line at Ballymoney there is a jewel, the three-foot gauge Ballycastle branch which has bogie *corridor* coaches still in LMS red and 2–4–2 Worsdell von Borries compound tanks. The coaches are leftovers from the unique narrow-gauge boat-trains from Larne to Ballymena, now but a memory. Close to Fair Head on the Antrim coast Ballycastle is a popular watering place in the summer, and seasonal traffic is heavy, so the line has not yet succumbed but

The three-foot gauge Londonderry & Lough Swilly Railway served some of the more isolated parts of Co Donegal and was effectively a main line as the remotest terminus was Burtonport, 74¼ miles from Derry. To work the train services the L&LS owned the only eight coupled narrow-gauge locomotives in Ireland, two 4–8–0 tender engines and two 4–8–4 tanks. No 6, one of the tanks built by Hudswell Clarke & Company of Leeds in 1912, is seen at Derry Pennyburn shed before the war. The railway finally closed in 1953 and No 6 lasted until closure.

The other narrow-gauge railway serving Co Donegal was the County Donegal Railways Joint Committee, jointly owned by the Great Northern Railway (Ireland) and Midland Railway of England and its successors. The CDR also traversed some wild country especially the climb to 591ft through the Barnesmore Gap between Stranorlar, its headquarters, and Donegal town. A return excursion from Ballyshannon hauled by a 2–6–4T is seen passing through the Barnesmore Gap on 3 August 1959.

time is not a friend. Even in the more prosperous north, Ireland is Ireland and less than a decade ago, in 1943, a train of two passenger coaches, ten wagons and a van ran away on the steep gradient dropping down into Ballycastle running through the buffer stops at the terminus, ending up in a stream on the other side of the road. No one was hurt.

Belfast is dour but the home of express trains. At Great Victoria Street station there are blue engines with teak stock to run over the Great Northern where, on the Dublin route, the dining cars have two separate locked cupboards of drinks for customs purposes. At York Road the Derby Moguls and Class 2 4–4–0s of the former LMS NCC, now the Ulster Transport Authority, go to Londonderry and the coast towns of Portrush and Larne, all with somersault semaphores. Last but certainly not least—for in its array of engines are a 2–4–0, 0–6–0s and an army of tanks—is the unique Belfast & County Down at Queens Quay. This is more like home, but an Irish home for all that.

The West Clare Railway was the longest three-foot gauge line, at 53 miles, inherited by the GSR and ran from Ennis to Kilrush and Kilkee. The line was dieselised in 1953/5 with four railcars, similar to CDR Nos 19 and 20, and three 0–4–0+0–4–0 locomotives but even this could not stave off closure which came in 1961. The WCR owned a total of 16 locomotives over the years and No 3c, originally named Ennistymon, was one of the last two engines built for the WCR by the Hunslet Engine Company of Leeds in 1922 and was withdrawn in 1953. No 3c is seen taking water at Ennis in 1950. The 5ft 3in line can be seen through the bridge.

25
ANOTHER ROUTE

ONE of the great joys of exploring Britain by train was that without extra cost your return journey could be by a different and much longer route. Even today there are plenty of opportunities for stretching a bargain, like going from the West Country to Paddington the direct way and stopping off at Swindon or Bristol on the return. But it is absolutely nothing like it used to be. With few exceptions, today there is a definite route and anything else is at least out of the ordinary and much slower. Many of the trains we loved ran on parallel routes for hundreds of miles, or even took journeys that crisscrossed each other, such as at Carlisle. Who among us went to Scotland and returned the same way?

Another route. Just say those two words and the brain automatically recalls the great alternatives of yesteryear and the fun we had deciding how to make the best of our opportunities. 'Another Route' was indeed a heading

The Great Central London extension was probably more useful as a cross-country route with its connection to the Great Western via Woodford and Banbury than an alternative route to London. Ex-GCR 4–6–0 LNER class B1 (later B18, following the introduction of the Thompson design in 1942) No 5196 is seen near Rothley in August 1931 with the Ports to Ports Express–Newcastle, Barry and Swansea.

Edinburgh was served by three routes from England: East Coast, West Coast and Waverley. The latter had through trains from St Pancras to Edinburgh and the day service in BR days was named The Waverley. The down train is leaving Leeds City North (formerly Wellington) c1959 hauled by Jubilee class 4–6–0 No 45694 Bellerophon.

liberally used in what might be described as the lazy Londoner's *Bradshaw*, the monthly *ABC Alphabetical Railway Guide*. Only being of use for journeys to or from the capital, and thus for practical purposes only for Londoners, it nevertheless had a substantial circulation and generations of hotel porters and individual travellers consulted it as the easiest way of seeing what was available. For enthusiasts, it usefully cited the fares for each route, 'Fares as above' of course implying you could return by the longer way for the same money.

Undoubtedly the most fortunate were those going from London north to places like Manchester, Edinburgh and Glasgow. Not only was their diversity of route but of restaurant-car trains as different as Catholic, C of E and Methodist. And while in many cases one route was quicker, there was often not much in it and one might anyway run at less convenient times. Or did we kid ourselves that the route we wanted to use was the one whose train left just as we would be ready?

To cite a few examples, Birmingham did have two nearly equal services until the London Midland's was effectively withdrawn to make way for the West Coast main line electrification, after which the Western was a very secondary alternative. Birmingham business folk swore allegiance to Paddington or Euston, and when two of different religion wanted to travel together it was like deciding whether the Catholic would go to the Methodist harvest festival or vice versa. Only perhaps in the Glasgow area were feelings more entrenched... and there it was as much about which way to take the daily train to work as making an occasional long-distance journey. If the North Eastern Railway showed what monopoly could achieve, then Glasgow suburban services epitomised the glory of competition.

If you had 'done' all three routes used by through trains, the London to Manchester journey was one that called for especial deliberation. Euston might have a grand entrance but before rebuilding was a pretty miserable station to depart from, and while the train itself would be fast and comfortable the scenery was not in the top league. Marylebone was a fun place to leave from, and the fact there were fewer opportunities to take ex-Great Central rails had to be taken into account. The end of the journey was spectacular, and since the completion of the first main-line electrification in Britain the journey through the long Pennine tunnel was no longer a pain; but having to share the exit from London with London Transport *was*, and the number of through services was limited. Against that, they tended to be less crowded, but the coaches could be dirty. The restaurant car was not as good: it was here we had been put in our place. The LNER did not serve Yorkshire pudding *and* horseradish. St Pancras was ever delightful. The train would be comfortable and the restaurant car probably the best, but it would be a short train and could be crowded. Again the later part of the journey was better, the passage through the Peak District indeed being grander than anything else on any of the routes. The train made more stops, seldom if ever missing Leicester, but Derby always gave a warm glow. Now, which way would you go tomorrow if you had to make the journey and all three routes were operating? For the writer it would have to be St Pancras.

For most railway lovers it would undoubtedly be St Pancras for Edinburgh or Glasgow, simply because that has been impossible for so many years. When everything was still open and running, the choice was not so obvious, for while you would never waste a passage of the Long Drag over the Settle & Carlisle reading, the extra time was very considerable. You could indeed only do the journey sensibly by the one daily through train each to Edinburgh (The Waverley) or Glasgow (The Thames–Clyde Express). But hold on; what is the hurry? Why not break the journey at Leeds… but then if you went from King's Cross you could do so at York, or if from Euston at Preston and take that promised visit to Blackpool. The choice was endless, and it came back to personal preference or your railway religion. We just count ourselves lucky we could take each route in turn, enjoying Shap and Beattock, the Pennines and the Long Drag, the cathedrals and East Coast.

There was nothing to stop you mixing and matching your own route. Glasgow St Enoch to Carlisle by the Glasgow & South Western line through

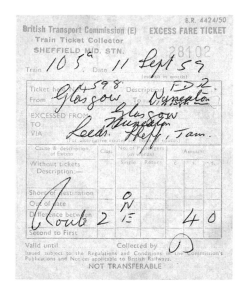

An excess ticket for the alternative route. Travel from Glasgow to Nuneaton via Leeds, instead of Crewe, cost this National Serviceman four shillings (20p) extra in 1959.

The LNER inherited two routes from London to Cambridge, one ex-Great Eastern from Liverpool Street and the other ex-Great Northern from King's Cross. The latter was probably the more popular and was served by express trains, some with buffet cars. Class 16/2 No 8787, one of the 'Royal Clauds' is passing Marshmoor with an up Cambridge on 25 May 1937. The stock appears to be five GN corridors with a non-corridor bringing up the rear but no buffet.

Above *The Midland & South Western Junction Railway was a cross-country line from Cheltenham (Lansdown) MR to Andover Junction LSWR and on over the LSWR to Southampton which fell into the GWR net in 1923. There were never any very fast trains this way but it provided a useful link, and between the wars there was a through coach from Liverpool to Southampton which was detached from the Pines Express at Cheltenham. In this view an ordinary passenger train from Andover to Cheltenham is leaving Cirencester Watermoor on 25 May 1953. GWR 4300 class 2–6–0 No 6384 is in charge.*

some of Scotland's finest non-barren scenery, to be savoured on a summer's evening after the LMS twelve-wheeler tea car came on at ugly Kilmarnock, and then south by the West Coast main line since it would be too dark to enjoy the Long Drag. But then through trains, especially sleepers serving Paisley, also performed that trick.

Cambridge was another place that had you alternating between routes, though generally the ambience of the buffet car expresses from King's Cross won. As for a journey between Cambridge and Oxford, the choice was between not doing it at all, finding an excuse to do it via London or somewhere else, or treat the wretched direct train as a joke. The Somerset & Dorset was altogether more businesslike than the link between the two great seats of learning. Many S&D journeys could of course equally well be taken via Southampton, but we loved the Joint Line and revelled in the fact that if you bought a ticket from Bridgwater to Paddington you could return from Waterloo via Templecombe... and occasionally save a minute or two on Western timings.

Sometimes we went from Marylebone out of homage to those who had put their faith in the Great Central, for here was a railway that hardly provided any journeys that could not be done equally well by another line. Faith indeed! We wondered what the hotel was like across the street at Marylebone when it welcomed the first passengers at the turn of the century, and despised the fact that, badly run down, it was now BR's headquarters. 222 Marylebone Road was a hateful address, for while much of BR was super, the overall policy was and became ever less attractive, culminating in Beeching's wretched 1963 report. The enquiry before the report had but one touch of joy: branch line closures were halted while it leisurely took place.

The Midland was one of three routes, all with through trains, between London and Manchester. It was also the most scenic as it traversed the heart of the Peak District. Jubilee class 4–6–0 No 45598 Basutoland awaits the right away with the 4.00pm Derby to St Pancras express in June 1955.

Opposite below *The Cheshire Lines Committee provided two alternative routes from Manchester, one to Chester and the other to Liverpool. A special empty coaching stock train is passing Knutsford c1949 hauled by LNER class J10 0–6–0 No 65161. All the CLC's passenger stock was non-corridor although some had internal lavatories.*

Great Western locomotives usually worked the West to North trains south of Hereford and/or Shrewsbury and Grange class 4-6-0 No 6861 Crynant Grange *is passing Abergavenny Junction with a northbound train in September 1952. Alongside the goods shed is an ex-LNWR 0-8-0 No 49168 fitted with tender cab for working the line to Merthyr.*

Opposite below *The LMS had an alternative route from London to Swansea via Stafford, Shrewsbury and Llandrindod Wells (Central Wales line) at the same fare as the direct route from Paddington. This anomaly was abolished with the rationalisation of fares in 1952. There was, and still is, a service from Shrewsbury to Swansea, and an ordinary passenger train from Shrewsbury is seen at Builth Road High Level, where the Central Wales crossed the Cambrian's Mid-Wales line from Moat Lane to Brecon. The locomotive is BR class 5 4-6-0 No 73025 allocated to Shrewsbury when that depot was coded 89A (1961-3).*

The era of the trains we loved ended along with many of their routes, certainly 'Another Route', with Beeching—the Great Central of course being a main casualty.

Glasgow to Edinburgh, Manchester to Leeds, Cardiff to Birmingham, London to Canterbury: we were not short of journeys where the choice could be sensibly made either way. But in practical terms one of the biggest choices was slightly different: whether to go cross-country or via London. From the West to Scotland that might involve leaving only an hour earlier for the same arrival time, and the exhilaration of a fast trip to and from the capital in exchange for the undoubted delights of a cross-country West to North service (still via Hereford and picturesque Ludlow of course) but the dubious pleasure of being shunted away from a platform during the Crewe stopover. If we were interested in locomotive performance, accelerations of the crack trains to the capital began to sway things, and soon the cross-countries were anyway a dying breed. You could no longer get from Devon to Folkestone with a single change at Reading (and that after arriving there by slip coach), and East Anglia lost most of its through services, including the restaurant car train that had taken the Joint line to Yarmouth and the Edinburgh–Cambridge service.

Cross-country trains had entirely their own aura. Few had the most recent rolling stock, and most stopped at all major traffic points where a considerable proportion of the passengers changed. It sometimes seemed that only you and the restaurant car crew remained the same. Many of these through trains had run at the same time for decades, being skilfully interwoven with services to or from London on successive routes to the capital.

But so had many branch-line services, and we must not forget that some journeys might involve taking a succession of all-station locals. One difficulty was discovering whether a return ticket was valid by our chosen deviation, as from Bristol to Aberystwyth out via Brecon and back via Carmarthen. If we could not do it by Monthly Return, the standard one-and-a-third times single rate, then there was always the Circular Ticket. That meant going to the local booking office and asking for a bespoke tour,

184

Above *South West and South Wales to North West trains were routed via the Severn Tunnel (from the South West) and Newport (from South Wales) then on to Hereford and Shrewsbury, the various portions joining at Pontypool Road. Here one such train, composed of a mixture of LMS and GW stock hauled by GW County class 4–6–0 No 1003* County of Wilts, *is seen near Llantilo Pertholey about one mile north of Abergavenny Junction on 11 September 1952.*

Above Brecon *was a jointly owned station and was served by four different railways, the Cambrian, Brecon & Merthyr, Neath & Brecon and Midland, prior to 1922. For many years the Midland worked the passenger trains over the Neath & Brecon to Colbren Junction which ran through from Hereford to Swansea St Thomas, providing an alternative route from Birmingham. The 6.20pm train for Neath (Riverside) on 9 August 1960 hauled by 5700 class 0–6–0PT No 9627 is about to depart.*

subject to an attractive discount. You had to give three days' notice. But then such journeys were usually planned over weeks if not months. The only problem was that if they were to happen near the beginning of the summer or winter timetable, you had no way of knowing whether traditional connections would continue to be maintained. In Ireland they seemed to insist on selling you tickets by routes that proved impractical and you were forever having an argument with one of the ticket collectors who seemed to appear with great regularity out of the bogs.

One other aspect of another route needs to be mentioned: the railway hotels. Mainly adjuncts to larger stations, they were railway institutions in their own right, in the days we are talking about almost invariably the best (outside London). Arriving in Glasgow by three different routes from England meant you could savour the delights of the showpieces of three former railways without going into the street.

26
INVERNESS–EUSTON

IF there is a single platform in the provinces that has seen greater drama than any other, it must surely be the longest, curved one at Inverness, No 2. That is where our Royal Highlander for London, a sitting, eating and sleeping train, waits while the sun is still high in the sky on a late August evening in 1959. We feel our own touch of drama as we check not only for our own but others' names on the lists of sleeping car berth allocations posted at the platform head. There is ours sandwiched between household names travelling second like us, though first class has a higher proportion of Honourables, Lords and Right Honourables.

As we walk two-thirds of the length of the platform to check in and deposit our baggage in our LMS two-berth sleeper, two Black Fives back onto the train... and we think of what has used this platform in bygone times. Always first to come to mind are those 'caravan trains' of pre-Grouping days, monstrous processions of carriages of many English and Scottish railways, each displaying a distinctive livery, along with a motley assortment of horse boxes and other four-wheeled conveyances of livestock and road carriages. Traditionally they arrived for the beginning of the grouse season on the Glorious Twelfth and departed two or three weeks later when the aristocracy had shot their quota of birds. On impulse we walk to the front van, and are not disappointed. Grouse addressed to the Claridge's and other top hotels and restaurants make you feel you are part of history... and there is a first-class passenger taking a brace into his twelve-wheeled LMS sleeper.

A lot of other history has been enacted on platform 2. For example, during two World Wars enormous contingents of military and naval people arrived and departed here, and we think of the heroic efforts made to keep exceptionally heavy traffic moving, especially by the Highland Railway in the 1914–18 war when the navy was based in the far north.

Our luggage in the sleeping compartment, we now claim our two window seats in a Mark 1 BR coach with superior wood fittings, but pause only momentarily to leave some personal belongings on the seat and move to our third position, in the restaurant car. 'First sitting', we are told forcibly, unable to determine whether second has sold out or the staff just insist on everyone eating early unless there is a genuine overflow. 'Take your seats on departure.'

Rather than return to our compartment (or sleeper) for the final ten minutes we walk around the romantic station, built on two sides of a triangle, the Rose Street curve completing it. When we arrived a couple of weeks ago, our train shot north along the curve and backed into this Templecombe of the North, supposedly to allow cross-platform connections to Wick/Thurso and Kyle of Lochalsh. Though, as we shall see, our train

Opposite below *During the summer many trains for Bournemouth were routed from the LMS system onto the Somerset & Dorset at Bath. Single line sections and the steep climb over the Mendips, requiring many trains to be double headed, gave the line a unique operational character. Here an up train from Bournemouth tackles the steep climb to Masbury summit at Winsor Hill with two S&D locomotives in charge on 23 August 1952. Class 7F 2–8–0 No 53802 (S&D No 82) leads the way with class 4F 0–6–0 No 44559 (S&D No 59) behind. Note the S&D passenger train headcode.*

supports a whole network of connections, passengers from the far North for the Royal Highlander would have arrived long ago, at 2.38pm, just after those from Kyle of Lochalsh. No doubt they have enjoyed afternoon tea in that Highland Railway showpiece, the Station Hotel. The evening trains from the North connect with the 'midnight', which has sleepers from Inverness to Edinburgh (recently introduced) and Glasgow—and even a through coach from Wick to Glasgow.

Not that the station is dull right now. Over on the far side at platform 7 is the last of the three daily departures for Kyle, due to leave at the same moment as us, while at platform 6 a small crowd is waiting to greet relatives and friends off the 10.00am from Glasgow, which is going to back in. At platform 3 the 6.00pm semi-fast to Aberdeen is beginning to load. Inverness has always enjoyed rush hours like this between long siestas, though even then the booking office is busy with people arranging the most complicated of journeys. The station's fascination is increased by the fact that most passengers are making journeys of several hours, some like ourselves of well over half a day. Yet the coat of arms of the Inverness & Nairn shows that the Highland capital's first railway was a purely local, self-contained affair.

Neither we nor the Kyle train leave at 5.40pm, for at 5.41, six minutes late, the 10.00 from Glasgow takes the Rose Street curve. It has not started to back in, to give a connection for Kyle, before we are given right away, and set off along the Firth under the magnificent signal gantries. Not so long ago the Euston sleeper started even earlier, a recent improvement being the introduction of an all-stations local to Aviemore, which allows us to run there non-stop.

Our Black Fives are allowed 62 minutes for the 34¾ miles mainly of hard climbing—a vast improvement on the last century when everything went via Forres. But the original road is still taken on Sundays and other days there is still a through section that way which we will pick up at Aviemore. It has a first- but no longer a second-class sleeper. We indeed saw it leave at 3.55pm at the back of an Aberdeen train. The through coaches are then scheduled to spend 30 minutes in Forres before being taken by a stopper to Aviemore, usually behind a 'Caley Bennie'; a number of these ex-Caledonian 4–4–0s, the equivalent to the ex-Highland Bens, are allocated to both Forres and Aviemore. But Black Fives are pretty ubiquitous on the Carr Bridge line and indeed services north from Inverness. The Black Fives are nicknamed Hikers by Highland enginemen. The nickname was presumably transferred from the ex-Great Eastern's B12s used on the Great North of Scotland section of the LNER and from the start were regular visitors to Inverness before Stanier introduced his 5P5Fs. For their respective railways, they were the first 4–6–0s imported from England to the Highlands.

So into the restaurant car for our four-course *table d'hôte* dinner, adequate but not as good as we are used to on the Western.

Occasionally the steam and smoke driven by an easterly breeze block our vision, but we make full use of the restaurant car's picture windows to soak in the scenery slowly passing by. A view of the Moray Firth and the whole Inverness area opens up as we climb up the 'new' line, and catch a glimpse of the prehistoric Clava Cairns from the viaduct. Bleak Culloden Moor and then rugged mountains. On the sharp curves we alternately see the Black

Fives toiling away and the train's rear.

We do not see another train till reaching Aviemore, but here there seems to be a gala display of activity, with several locomotives on shed, the first part of our train with its first-class sleeper at the other face of the island platform waiting to be joined to us, and clearly an important down arrival expected—which rolls in two minutes early with another pair of Black Fives on its way from Perth to Inverness. The main restaurant portion goes the direct route while three coaches are detached to run via Forres, taking an extra seventy minutes to Inverness, the Caley Bennie we saw on the turntable perhaps going to take charge. We note that the Perth train has already shed one section, at Ballinluig for Aberfeldy. A short goods train has a single Black Five waiting to follow us. There is life aplenty in the Highlands, but soon the diesels will be coming and it will all change.

We are allowed fifteen minutes at Aviemore but leave a few late. The two Black Fives however seem determined to make light work of the load that has been increased to sixteen bogies, a snake that will be watched by a high proportion of the not very many people living along the next section of route of glorious scenery beside loch, through gaps in the mountains and ultimately a gorge before the summit is reached. Now we stop almost everywhere, picking up two or three people at Kincraig, Kingussie, Newtonmore, Dalwhinnie with its distillery, but miss Struan though we note it is important enough to be a starting point for a morning train to Perth. We of course stop at Blair Atholl, starting point for three services to Perth already dieselised, and at Pitlochry by which time it is dark.

Long back in our compartment, we have stayed up hoping to catch a glimpse of the Pass of Killiecrankie, but fail. So feeling a little conspicuous, we say good night to our envious companions who will sit all the way to Euston (no doubt making good use of our vacated seats) and also to our sleeping car attendant and 'retire' for the night. Or at least that was the intention, but before we have undressed we stop at Dunkeld & Birnam ('Stops on notice to take up for England', says our timetable; the solitary gent must feel important halting us) and are still not settled when nearly half an hour later, a few minutes early, we roll into Perth. In truth we have been reading a collection of excursion and other leaflets taken from Inverness booking office and dipping into the timetable, noting that with the improvements of the last few years there are now a dozen named Anglo-Scottish expresses. Those running within Scotland include the Fife Coast Express from Glasgow to St Andrews as well as the Granite City, the Saint Mungo and the Bon Accord on the Glasgow–Aberdeen run.

Having told our steward that we will not want a breakfast tray, the spirit of adventure overcomes us and we change our mind. After an early dinner it is going to be a long night, and we notice that passengers joining up to Perth can order breakfast to be delivered after Rugby. We even buy a bar of Nestlé's milk chocolate which we nibble while the restaurant car goes off. It will do breakfast service on the return working in the morning. Then to the spacious toilets also being visited by a few others off the train, regular passengers who obviously know what is best. Perth's own sleeper (that involved in the Harrow & Wealdstone disaster) has already left, but we see a local in from Dundee Tay Bridge and what seem to be endless shunting

189

movements. Again we leave late, catching a glimpse of the 8.15pm diesel from Glasgow Buchanan Street to Dundee. It is still two and a half hours before the 1.25 restaurant car from Euston to Perth arrives, running most of the way behind the mid-day Scot which will have picked up a through Glasgow coach from Plymouth. The more you learn and remember, the more you want to consult your timetable: it is called compulsion. Constantly one has to remember the Scottish Region arranges tables outward from Glasgow and Edinburgh first and then to them, so first comes Glasgow to Carlisle.

We wish it were daylight to enjoy the complications of the Stirling to Motherwell main line, and certainly we wonder why we as well as Perth's own sleeper stop at Coatbridge (Central), apparently an important traffic point. But by now we are dozing off, if not deeply asleep.

We just regain consciousness at Carlisle and Crewe, more on account of snippets of conversation from the porters pushing barrows than the actual stop. Nuneaton (Trent Valley) we miss entirely, but a couple from a neighbouring cabin decide it is time we were all awake as they chirp away in the corridor on the approach to Rugby, and we hear that familiar sleeping car sound coming from the pantry at the coach's end, the tinkling of teacups being laid out. Half an hour later our breakfast tray appears; we eat it and still wish there were a restaurant car to go to for another!

We have been running fast much of the night, but now engineering work and no doubt other trains running out of sequence cause a series of delays and we see several trains carrying workers to London overtake us on the slow line while we stop and start on the fast. Maybe they are allowing some of the locals onto the main line ahead of us, the circumstance that led to the Perth sleeper crash at Harrow & Wealdstone. But this morning is bright and there is no fear of our driver passing signals. Indeed, he seems to slam on the brake at the first sight of a distant at caution.

And so we drop down the bank and through the tunnels into Euston, fifteen minutes late at 8.50am, 15 hours 10 minutes after leaving Inverness. It has indeed been a long, hungry night but at least we caught some sleep lying down and are surprised at how sprightly the majority who have sat up all night walk along the platform.

Auto-Train Appeal

Among the trains we most loved were the push-pull auto-car ones that mainly ran on branch lines and had a culture entirely of their own. None yet runs in preservation but as Patron of the South Devon Railway Association I am appealing for funds to restore GWR 0–4–2T No 1420 and an auto-car with working push-pull equipment. If you have fond memories of the Trains We Loved, please send a donation: David St John Thomas, Patron's Auto-Train Fund, South Devon Railway Association, Buckfastleigh Station, Buckfastleigh, South Devon.

DStJT

INDEX

Aberdeen, 94, 149, 152, 156, 188, 189
Aberystwyth, 30, 184
Accidents, 28, 81, 82, 92, 163, 174;
 Abermule, 88; Harrow & Wealdstone, 82,
 163, 189, 190
Adams radial tanks, *50*
Anderson, Bill, 157
Arigna branch, 174, *176*
Ashchurch, *82*
Atherstone, *123*
Atlantics, 8B 'Jersey Lily', *146*; Z, *146*, 147
Auto-cars, 112, 126
Automatic Train Control, 27, 163
Aviemore, 188, 189

B1 4–6–0 *Strang Steel, 154–5*
Badminton, *20*
Ballinamore, 174, 176
Ballycastle line, 177, 178
Baltic tanks, 169
Banks, 42, 48, 112; Beattock, *78*, 142, *158*,
 181; Campden, *17, 21*; Dainton, 25, 109,
 113; Gelnagalt, 174; Goodrington Sands,
 29; Gravelly Hill, 49; Hatton, *6*;
 Hemerdon, 109; Hopton, 164; Wellington,
 109
Bar/tavern cars, 93, 140
Barnard Castle, *131*
Barnesmore Gap, 177, *178*
Basingstoke, *62*, 116
Belfast, 168, 178; Great Victoria Street, 178;
 Queen's Quay, 178; York Road, 178; –
 Cork, 170; – Londonderry, 172, 177, 178;
 & County Down Railway, 169, 178
Belturbet, 174, 176
Bennett, Arnold, 69
Birkenhead, 30, 88–9, 116
Birmingham, 30, 32, 69, 116, 126, 132, 180;
 New Street, *7, 10–11, 12, 14*, 42, *43*, 47,
 49, 69, *73*, 83, 99; Snow Hill, *6*, 12, 30,
 69, *71*, 99, 116, 127; – Bristol, 12, *18*; –
 Glasgow, *78*; – Penzance, 12; suburban
 services, 42–52, *44, 45, 49*
Black Five 4–6–0s, *10–11*, 90, 119, 126, 187
Blackpool, 79, 82, *118*, 120, 132, 181
Boat trains, *22*, 35, 53, *57*, 60, 61, 101, 120,
 149, 177–8; Golden Arrow, 9, 59, 61;
 Night Ferry, 61
Bon Accord, 189
Bookstalls, 66–7, 69
Bournemouth, 61, 116, 132; Belle, *17*, 61, *62*
BR, 12, 16, 18, 21, 26, 27, 101, 116, 118,
 120, 123, 129, 145, 152, 157, 160, 167,
 183
Bradford, 12, 37, 116, 132
Brakes, 13, 27, 30, 64, 152, 160
Branch lines, 13, 16, 34–5, 82, 94, 111–17,
 130–3, *131*, 135, 153, 157, 169, 173, 174,
 184 *see also individual entries*
Brecon, 184, *186*; & Merthyr Railway, 186
Brighton, 56, 116; Belle, 22, 61
Bristol, 12, 109, 179, 184; Parkway, 23;
 Temple Meads, *2*, 74; & Exeter Railway,
 109
Bristolian, *2*
Broadsman, 101
Buchan line, 35, 156
Buffet cars, 24, 70, 101, 181, 183
Bulleid, Oliver, 24, 60 *see also* Pacifics
Bundoran, 177; Express, 168
Burton-on-Trent, 116, 126

Caledonian Railway, 148, 149, 152–3
Callander & Oban Railway, 153
Cambrian Coast, 87; Express, *6*, *121*;
 Railway, 88, 90, 186
Cambridge, 101, 181, 183, 184; – Oxford,
 183
Camwell, Arthur, 164, 167
Cardiff, – Birmingham, 184; – Plymouth, *23*
Carlisle, 79, 152, 179, 181, 190; – Newcastle,
 152; – Stranraer, 152
Car carriers, 116, 133, 152
'Caravan trains', 187
Carmarthen, 81, 184
Castle 4–6–0s, 25, 27, 30, 90, 99; *Beaufort, 2*;
 Cardigan, 39; *Carew, 112*; *Clun, 106–7*;
 Lamphey (Sir Edward Elgar), 126; *Lydford,
 65*; *Monmouth, 17*; *Neath Abbey, 113*;
 Sudeley, 121; *Swordfish, 23*; *Tenby, 99*;
 Thornbury, 25, 110, *110*
Catch pits, *164*, 166
Cathcart Circle, 143
Cattle trains, 32, 56, 69, *161*, 162, 168, *168*,
 173–4, 177
Cavan & Leitrim Railway, 174, 176
Charing Cross 40, 60
Cheltenham, 27, 99, 182
Chester, 88, 89, 183
Children, 32, 38–41, 85, 141
Chipping Norton, *27*
Circus trains, 41
Class 5 2–6–0s, *87*, *125*; 4–6–0s, *80*, 85, 86,
 185, 188
Cleanliness, 22, 31, 81, 82, 141, 145
Closures, 13, 82, 100, 104, 163; Beeching,
 16, 59, 152, 183–4
Coaches, 21–4, 30, 86, 172, 176; 'concertina'
 corridor, *84*; Mark Is, *25*, *99*, *123*, 187,
 IIIs, *19*, 77; non-corridor, 60, 74, 76, 82,
 86, *87*, 112, 114, 135, 183; saloons, 172;
 slip, 13; with balconies, 176
Coal trains, 35–6, 79, 94, 125, 134, 149
Commuter traffic, 34, 36, 45, 53, 56, 94, 96,
 149
Compound 4–4–0s, 43, 47; *Eagle, 169*
Coras Iompair Eireann (CIE), 170, 174
Cork, Blackrock & Passage Railway, 176
Coronation, 20; Scot, *19*, 20, 149
Cornishman, 12–13, 25, 27, 99, 101, 105,
 106–7, 109, 112
County 4–6–0s, *Somerset, 84*; *Wilts, 185*
County Donegal Railways, 170, 172, 173,
 176–8 *passim*
Coventry, 79, 87
Crewe, 72, 83, 89, 126, 184, 190
Croagh Patrick, 162
Cromford & High Peak Railway, 164–7
Cross-country services, *23*, 27, 32, 34, 116,
 132, 152, 179, 182, 184 *see also individual
 entries*

D49/2 4–4–0 *Albrighton, 74*
Darlington, 132, *146*
Dawlish, 101, *102–3*, 105, 120
Delays, 32, 41, 48–9, 70, 72, 74–6, 86, 120,
 190
Deltics, 24, 100, 104, 128, 133–4, 152; *Green
 Howards, 104*
Depots *see* Sheds
Derby, 79, *125*, 126–7, 181; – St Pancras, *183*
Devon Belle, *61*
Devonian, 37, 132

Diesels/dieselisation, 28, 30–1, 61, 62, *79*, 83,
 100, 128, *129*, 132, 134, 152, 189; *Cossack,
 41*; *Sir Edward Elgar*, 31
Director 4–4–0 *Somme*, 127
Diversions, 86–7, 132
Docks, 100, 101, 134; Immingham, 101, 104;
 Tyne, *130*
Double-heading, 53, 79, 118, 164, 174
Dover, 9, 22, 133
Dromod, 174, 176
Drummond, Dugald, 51
Drummond T9 4–4–0s (Greyhounds), *51*, 53
Dublin, 168, 176, 177; Amiens Street, *170*,
 171; Area Rapid Transit (DART), 174;
 Westland Row, 171; – Belfast, 168–70,
 172; – Cork, 172
'Dukedog' 4–4–0s, 16, ;90
Dudley, 126
Dundalk, Newry & Greenore Railway, 169,
 172

East Anglia, 24, 94, *95*, 97, 100, 101, 161,
 184; Region, 100
East Coast main line, 83, *95*, 97, *98*, 100,
 104, 128, 133, 145, 147, 152
Eastern Region, 100, 101, 104
Edinburgh, 134, 148, 149, 152, 156, 180;
 Princes Street; 148; Waverley, 68, *144*, 149,
 152; – Cambridge, 184; – King's Cross,
 129, 133, *145*, 156, 181
Electrification, 12, 53, 56, 57, 83, 100, 148,
 152, 180, 181
Elizabethan, 68, 133, *133*, *145*
Elliot, John, 60
Ellis, Hamilton, 9, 16
Enniskillen, 173, 174, *178*
Euston, 34, 79, 80, 82, 83, 86, 88, *139*, 190; –
 Birmingham, 86, 180; – Glasgow, 12, *19*,
 81, 181; – Manchester, 12, *77*, *147*, 181;
 – Wolverhampton, *10–11*, 21
Excursions, 12, *14*, 39, 60, 72, 74, 82, 85, *87*,
 96, 120, 134–6, 152, 177, *178*
Exeter, 60, 133; St David's, 26, 60, 70, 109,
 112, 117; St Thomas, 120
Expresses, 22–3, 69–70, 81, 83, 96–7, 100,
 123, 132, 151; Anglo-Scottish, 69, *78*, 134,
 149, 189, 'Goods', *158*; Atlantic Coast, 57,
 60, 61; Cornish Riviera, 61, 70, 101,
 105–14; Emerald Isle, 123; Enterprise,
 168, *170*; Fife Coast, 189; Lakes; 120;
 North Atlantic, 174; Pines, *71*, 182; Ports
 to Ports, 27, 132, *179*; 'Royal Clauds', *181*;
 Thames–Clyde, 132, 149, 152, 181;
 Torbay, 70, 101; West to North, 90

Fares, 24, 48, 85, 96, 180, 184, 186; supple-
 mentary, 94
Filey, 116, 132, 133
Fish trains, 35, 94, 133, 156
Flower trains, 84–5
Flying Scotsman, 70, 94, 129, 130, 132
Forbes, Henry, 176
Forres, 188, 189
Freight traffic, 12, 16, 33, 35–6, *44*, 61, 84,
 93–4, 96, 100, 133, 149, 157, 159–62,
 171, 176, *see also individual entries*; trains,
 28, 30, *30*, *82*, *83*, 94, 96, 96, *111*, 126,
 127, 137, *142*, 152, 157–60, *161*, 177,
 'Cauliflower' 0–6–0s, 47, *122*, Dean, *160*,
 162, pick-up, 13, 126, 152, 'Scotch', *158*,
 159, Super D 0–8–0s, 90, 123, *124*
Fruit/vegetable trains, 35, 84, 120, 161, 177

Gas Turbine locomotive, *160*
Gateshead, *98*, 133–4
Glasgow, 12, 81, 132, 142–9, 152, 156, 180,
 181, 186; Buchanan Street, 149; Central,
 66, 142–3, 145, *149*; Queen Street, 148; St
 Enoch, 148–9, 152, 181; Subway, 148;
 – Aberdeen, 152, 189; – Carlisle, 190;
 – Edinburgh, 184; – Oban, 142, 149, 152;
 – Plymouth, 149; – St Andrews, 189; &
 South Western Railway, 149, 152, 181
Gourock, 149; express, 143
Grand, Keith, 26
Grantham, 70, *98*
Grange 4–6–0 *Crynant, 184*
Granite City, 189
Great Central Railway, 79, 94, 100, 126, 132,
 145, 179, 183–4
Great Eastern Railway (Jazz service), 94, 100,
 188
Great North of Scotland Railway, 149, 153,
 156, 188
Great Northern Railway, 94, 100, 159;
 (Ireland), 168, 169, 172–4, 176–8, *passim*
Great Southern Railway, 170–2 *passim*; &
 Western, 171, 173
Great Western Railway, 7, 19, 25–31, 57, 61,
 66, 70, 74, 88–90, 100, 115, 121, 135,
 145, 179, 182
Gresley, Sir Nigel, 96, 97 *see also* Pacifics
Greenore, 169, *172*
Grouping, 9, 12, 19, 79–80, 94, 129, 149

Halts, 31, 82; Watergate, 56
Hall 4–6–0s, 90; *Acton Burnell, 71*; *Berrington,
 33*; *Croxteth, 89*
Haulage, atmospheric, 105, 112; chain,
 165–7; horse, 169, 174
Hawkins, Philip, 13
Hayling Island line, *52*
Heating, 36, 157
Heart of Midlothian, 132
Hereford, 88, 90, 184–6 *passim*
High Speed 125s, 104, 109
Highland Railway, 187
Holiday traffic, 12, *14*, 16, *29*, 33–5, 53, *54–5*,
 60, *63*, 72, 85–7, 97, 101–16, *102–3*,
 106–7, *112*, *129*, 177
Holyhead, 78, 132, 169
Honeymooners, 37
Hotels, 78, 81, 142, 148, 183, 186, 188
Hull, 101, 116, 130

Inclines, 13, 160, 164–6, *164*; Lickey, *83*, 119
InterCity, 80, 83, 120
Intermediate 2–4–0s, *95*
Inverness, 133, 156, 187–8; – Euston,
 187–90; & Nairn Railway, 188
Ireland, 120, 132, 162, 168–78, 186
Isles of Scilly, 84, 116

Jubilee 4–6–0s, 9, 89; *Atlas, 123*; *Basutoland,
 183*; *Bellerophon, 180*; *Novelty, 21*;
 Polyphemus, 10–11; *Trafalgar, 14*
Jumbo 2–4–0s, 47
Junctions, 66, 83, 91, 108; Abergavenny, *184*;
 Barmouth, *15*; Buttington, 88, 90; Cairnie,
 153; Church Road, 42, 43; Cogload, 109;
 Colbren, 186; Colwich, *122*; Corianlarich,
 152–3; Cowley Bridge, 109; Evercreech,
 54–5; Ferryhill, *143*; Fintona, 169, 174;
 Halwill, *51*, 56; Harborne, 48, Hatton
 North, 99; Killin, 153; Limerick, 171,

Moyasta, 174; Pontsticill, *28*; Rolleston, 163; Thingley, *26*, *84*, *160*; Tiverton, 109; Tooban, 177; Tyseley, 99, 109; Wortley, *131*

K2 2–6–0 *Loch Rannoch*, 153
King 4–6–0s, 25, 26, 30, 89, 108; *Edward II*, *102–3*; *George V*, 26; *Henry III*, *113*; *James I*, *108*; *James II*, 6; *Richard III*, 6
King's Cross, 12, *12*, 24, 86, *93*, 94, 100, 101, *150–1*, *158*; – Cambridge, 101, 181, *181*, 183; – Edinburgh, *104*, 129, 132, 133, *145*, 156, 181; – Glasgow, 12, *132*; – Leeds and Bradford, *12*
King's Norton, *45*
Kingswear branch, 13, *29*, 109
Kirkby Stephen, 116, *134*
Kitchen cars, 34, *141*
Knowle & Dorridge, *99*
Kyle of Lochalsh, 187, 188

Lake District, 79, 82
Lancashire & Yorkshire Railway, 79, 83
Leeds, 12, 116, 130, 132, *180*, 181
Leicester, 66, 69, 126, 181
Level crossings, 61, 70, 134, 169
Liveries, 26, 30–1, 79, 83, 100, 112, 118, 121, 145, 169, 173
Liverpool, 24, 60, 79, 116, 183; – Southampton, 182
Liverpool Street, 24, 67, 94, 96, 100, 101, 104, 162; – Cambridge, 181; – Norwich, 101
LMS, 20, 30, 34, 45, 77–82, 96, 138, 141, 149, 152, 174
LNER, 20, 66, 94–7, *95*, *98*, 100, 129, 130, 149, 152, 159, 181, 188
LNWR, 45–8, 79, 83, 147, 165, 169, 172
London, 23, 61, 70, 74, 81, 134, 180, 184 *see also individual termini*;
– Barrow–Workington, 122; – Canterbury, 184; – Manchester, 181, 183; – Swansea, 184; – Brighton, & South Coast Railway, 53, 56; – Midland Region, 82–3, 116; – & North Western Railway, 50, 56, 182; North – Railway, 164, 167
Londonderry, 172, 174, 176–8; & Enniskillen Railway, 174, *175*; & Lough Swilly Railway, 173, 177
Lord Nelson 4–6–0 *Howard of Effingham*, 22
Luggage, 23; PLA, 13, 32, 40, 85, 119, 137
Lyme Regis branch, *50*

Machines, automatic, 67, 89
Mail trains, 32–3, *143*, 152; TPOs, 13, 32
Management, 56, 57, 60, 80, 96–7, 100, 132
Manchester, 12, 79, 83, 94, 96, 112, 116, 126, 180, 181, 183, – Chichester, 183; – Leeds, 184; – Liverpool, 183; – Paignton, *112*
Mancunian, 77, 123
Manor 4–6–0s, 4, 16, 90, *119*, *Foxcote*, 15, *Fritwell*, *136*
Maps, 66, *132*, *156*
Marylebone, 83, 94, 132, 145, 171, 183; – Edinburgh, 152; – Manchester, 12, 96, 181
Maunsel, R.E.L., 63
Mayflower, 26, 101
Meals, 24, 34, 70, 101, 112, 119, 138–41, 156, 188; breakfast, 22, 138–40 *passim*, 189, 190; coffee, 24, 38, 139; dinner, 101, 188; tea, 112, 138–40 *passim*
Merchant Venturer, *160*
Middleton Top, 164–7, *166*
Midland, 18, 77, 79, 83, 178, 180, 183, 186; & Great Northern, 104, 116; & Great Western, 14, 173; & South Western Junction, *182*
Midlander, *10–11*, *21*
Milk traffic, 35, 65, 69, 84, 97, 162
Moguls, 16, 90, *90*, 109, 136, 169–70, 172, 178

Narrow gauge, 16, 165, 170, 172–4, 176
Nationalisation, 9, 13, 16, 20–1, 82, 89, 100, 116, 129–30, 132, 152, 169; anti– 100
Neath & Brecon Railway, 186

Newcastle, 130, 132–4, *133*, 152; – Swansea, 132
Newport, 23, 185
'Newspaper trains', *113*
Non-stop runs, 22–3, 70, 109, 112, 114, 116–17, 129, 130, 132, 133, *145*, 168
Norfolkman, 67
Norseman, 132
North British Railway, 148, 149, 152, 156
North Briton, 132
North Devon & Cornwall Junction Railway (Withered Arm), *51*, 56, *56*, *59*, 61
North East Region, 100, 129–34, 152
North Eastern Railway, 94, 129, 130, 147
North Warwickshire line, 99
Northern Counties Committee, 169, 172, 174, 177, 178
Northumbrian, 132
Nuneaton, *124*, 190

Oban, 140, 149, 152, 156
Observation cars, 152
Outings, school, 38–40, *39*, *41*, 72
Overnight services, 32, 34, 35, 116, 133, 134, 152, 156 *see also* Sleepers
Oxford, 116, 183

Pacific 4–6–2s, 24, 57, 60–1, 83, 89, 90, 100; Battle of Britain class, 61, *Squadron*, *57*, *58*, *Lord Beaverbrook*, *73*; Britannia class, 24, 89, 101, *Lord Hurcomb*, 67, *Iron Duke*, *59*, *William Shakespeare*, 8; Class 7 *Shooting Star*, *20*; Coronation class, 124, *Princess*, 128, *Princess Margaret Rose*, *78*, *Duchess of Montrose*, *158*; Duchess class, 89; Gresley A1 *St Simon*, *95*, A2 *A.H. Peppercorn*, *143*, A3 *Flying Scotsman*, 97, *Tranquil*, *98*, *White Knight*, *131*, A4, 24, 96–7, 100, 128, 133, *133*, 152, *Kingfisher*, 68, *Mallard*, *93*, *98*, *145*, *Miles Beevor*, *12*, *Quicksilver*, *150–1*, *Woodcock*, *12*; Merchant Navy class 60, 61, *Blue Funnel*, 61, *Blue Star*, 17, *Cunard White Star*, 58; Princess Royal class, 61, 75, *City of Wells*, 58, *Lady Patricia*, *138*; West County class, 61, *City of Wells*, 58, *Combe Martin*, *54–5*, *Dorchester*, 62, *Salisbury*, 62
Paddington, 20, 23–6, *passim*, 28, 30, 31, 65, 74, 86, 88, *110*, 179, 180, 183; – Birkenhead, 89; – Bristol, *26*, 179; – Penzance, 25, *25*; – Plymouth, 25, *113*, 117; – St Ives, 105–14
Paignton, 37, 112, 132
Pannier tanks, *2*, *15*, 27, 28, 119
Patriot 4–6–0s, 7; *Derbyshire Yeomanry*, *2*, *14*; *Royal Pioneer Corps*, *7*
Peak class 45 1Co-Co1, *104*
Peak District, 82, 164–6, 181, 183
Penzance, 12, 25, 116
Peppercorn A1 *Osprey*, *150–1*
Perth, 69, 152, 156, 189
Peterborough, 10, 127–8; – Yarmouth, 104
Peters, Ivo, 53, 120
Piloting, 13, 42, 119, 136, *144*
Plymouth, 25, 109, 117, 149
Posters, 66, 78–9, 97, *97*
Prairie tanks, 16, 28, *28*, *110*, 112, 114, *114*, 135, 136, 162
Precursor 4–4–0 *Tamerlane*, *147*
Preston, 69, 82, 120, 181
Prince of Wales 4–6–0 *Queen of the Belgians*, 89
Pull-and-push services, *81*, *163*
Pullmans, 13, *17*, 22, 53, 61, *61*, *62*, *73*, 83, 132, 134, 140; Queen of Scots, 132; Sunday, 132; Tees-Tyne, *93*, 132, *150–1*; Yorkshire, 132
Pwllheli, 119, 120

2–6–0 *Queen Elizabeth*, *175*

Railcars, 168, *170*, 176, 178
Railway Magazine, 24, 67
Raven, Sir Vincent, 147
Reading, 23, 108, 184
Red Dragon, *20*; Rose, 123

Refreshment rooms, 65–7 *passim*, 69, 70, 72, 89, 153
Restaurant cars, 20, 22, 34, 38, 70, 76, 101, 115, 119, 125, 132, 138–41, *139*, 149, 157, 173, 180, 181
Robinson, J.G., 145
Rolt, L.T.C., 172
Royal Duchy, 25, *25*, 26, 101; Highlander, 187, 188; Scot, 123; Scot class, 78, 81, *Queen's Westminster Rifleman*, 77
Rubery, 15
Rugeley, 122, 123, 125–6; – Stourport, 87
Runaways, 164, 166, 176, 178
'Runners', 70

Safety, 27, 92, *see also* Accidents
Saint Mungo, 189
Saturday traffic, 12, *14*, 60, 72, 74, 105, 114–20, *117*, 132, 137, 157, 168
Scarborough, 97, 116, 120, *129*, 132–4 *passim*; Flyer, 132
School 4–4–0s, 63; *Charterhouse*, 63; *Clifton*, 60
School trains, 40–1, 72
Scotland, 34–6 *passim*, 78, 79, 83, 94, 142–56; Region, 100, 152, 190
Sea Wall, 30, 105, *113*
Selby, John, 43
Settle & Carlisle Railway (Long Drag), 83, 181, 183
Shamrock, 123
Sheds/Depots, 62, 81, 128, 162; Ballinamore, 174, 176; Barrow Road, Bristol, 7; Basingstoke, 62; Bushbury, 9; Exmouth Junction, 59; Gateshead, *98*; Glanmire Road, Cork, *171*; Laira 109; Middleton Top, *167*; Monument Lane, Birmingham, 32, 47, 49; Neasden, 100, *146*; Newton Abbot, 163; Nine Elms, *58*; Pennyburn, Londonderry, 177, *177*; Stafford, 123; Stewarts Lane, Battersea, 8, 59, *59*; St Ives, *114*; St Margarets, Edinburgh, *154–5*; Weybridge, 61
Sheffield, 69, 94, 116, 126
Ships, 12, 60, 78, 169
Shrewsbury, 4, 88–9, *89*, *121*, 184, 185
Shunting, 13, 28, 46, 48, *61*, 69, 70, *82*, *89*, *118*, *130*, *134*, 153, *153*, 167, 183, *186*
Signals, 13, *13*, *15*, 27, 34, 43, 56, 69, 70, *82*, 88, *118*, 122, *124–6*, *125*, 130, *131*, 134–7; bells, 36, 65, 66; boxes, *17*, 34, 56, 66, 117, *123*, *133*, 135, 137
Sleepers, 34, 86, 116, 132, 133, 152, 156, 183, 187, 188, 190
Sligo, Leitrim & Northern Counties Railways, 170, 173
Somerset & Dorset Railway, 53, *54–5*, *81*, 116, 120, 126
South Eastern & Chatham Railway, 56
South Yorkshireman, 132
Southampton, 60, 120, 182, 183
Southern Railway, 24, 25, 53–63, 140
Specials, 32, 34, 37, 60, 72, 81, 91, 126, 166, *166*, 171; banana, 84; cattle, 162; educational, 37, 39, *39*, *104*; hop pickers, 60, 161; postal, 32; Starlight, 116, 152; sporting, 37, 72, football, 37, 85–6, racing, 37, 86; VIPs, 53
Speed, 13, 23, 24, 60, 86, 97, 100, 108, 109, 119, 136, 174
Sprinters, 23
Stamp, Lord, 80, 81
Stanier, Sir William, 80, 81, 188
Starcross, 105, *106–7*
Stations, 9, 13, 31, 64–74, 77, 78, 81; staff, 24, 26, 68–9, 85, 88–9, 93–4, 130
Steamers, paddle, 104, 143, 148; *Lincoln Castle*, 101
St Erth, 111, 114
St Ives, *110*, 114, *114*
Stockton & Darlington Railway, 130
St Pancras, 20, 79, 82, 83; – Edinburgh, 132, 180, 181; – Glasgow, 12, 152, 181; – Manchester, 12, 83, 181, 183

Strabane, 176, 177
Stranorlar, 176, 177
Stranraer, 132, 152
Sugar beet traffic, 93–4, 97, 100, 161
Summits, Masbury, *186*; Shap, *138*, 142, 181; Whiteball, *39*
Sunday services, 34, 60, 86, 115, 120
Swansea, 132, 184, 186; – Penzance, 25
Swindon, 23, 30, 33, 132, 179; – Bristol, *84*

Tailte 4–6–0, *170*
Talisman, 132
Teignmouth, 9, 105, *113*
'Terrier' tank, *52*
Thanet/Kentish Belle, *73*
Thompson, Edward, 154
Through the Window, 109
Tickets, *173*; Circular, 184, 186; excess, *181*; platform, 67–8; Regulation, 119; Runabout, *116*, 120, 132, 156, *156*; season, 45
Timetables, 24, 96, 115–18, 132, 141, 143, 156, 173, 190; *ABC*, 180; *Bradshaw*, 115
Token exchangers, 13, 16, 135–7 *passim*
Track, 30, 78, 83, 86, 100
Tralee & Dingle Railway, 168, 170, 173–4
Trams, 142, 169
Treacy, Bishop, 100
Trent Valley line, 122–8, *122*, *124*
Tunnels, 42, 105, 164; Mountfield, *60*; Mutley, 109; Parsons, 9, *30*; Penge, *57*; Pennine, 181; Severn, 185; Whiteball, 109
Turntables, 45–7 *passim*
Tynesider, 132

Ulster, 80, 152, 169, 172, 176–8; Transport Authority, 172, 178
Uppingham, *13*

Valentia Harbour branch, 173
Valve gear, 64, 89, 94
Veltom, Oliver, 88
Viaducts, Dawlish, 105; Dowery Dell, *14*; Langston, 53; Largin, *29*; Owencarrow, 177; St Germans, 112
Victoria, *22*, 61, *73*; – Dover, *22*

Waiting rooms, 36, 46, 48, 65, 66, 69, 72
Wales, Central, 90, 185, *185*; North, 79, 82, 94, 120; South, *28*, 78, 185, – Paddington, *20*, 23, 24; *see also* Cambrian
Walker, Sir Herbert, 56–7
Warship diesels, 2, 28, 29, *29*, 41
Watering, *10–11*, *85*, 86–7, 116, *144*, *147*, 168, 174, *178*; troughs, 60, 86, 147
Waterloo, 53, 56, *63*, 120, 183; – Bournemouth, *17*; – Lymington Pier, *63*
Waverley, 132, 152, *180*, 181
Weather, 35–6, *59*, 157; floods, 87, 132; fog, 32, 162–3; snow, 36–7, 87, fences, *142*
Wells, *81*
Welshpool, 88, 90, *90*
Wenford Bridge line, *56*, 61
West Clare Railway, 172, 174, 178
West Coast main line, 79, *79*, 83, 152, 180, 183
West Highland Railway, 152–3, 156
West Riding Limited, 20, 132
Western Region, 9, 13, 25–31, 74, 105–14, 162, 164
Weymouth, 30, 61; – Swindon, *33*
Whale, George, 147
Whisky traffic, 35, 133
White Rose, *12*, 132
Wolverhampton, 4, 9, 12, 25, 89, 127
Works, 86, 96; Cowlairs, 156; Swindon, 31, 41, *41*, 127
World War I, 19, 187; II, 9, 12, 16, 20, 32, 60, 100, 169

Yards, freight, 35, 42, 46, 48, 93, 123, 135, 160–1; marshalling, 12, 137, 157, 162, Washwood Heath, *159*
Yarmouth, 104, 184
York, 69, *74*, 104, *104*, *117*, 120, 129, 130, 134, 152, 181